No Bull
Barre Chords
For Guitar

Learn and Master the Essential Barre Chords that all Guitar Players Need

by James Shipway

No Bull Barre Chords for Guitar
by James Shipway

Published by Headstock Books
headstockbooks.com

Book Cover Design by ebooklaunch.com

Paperback ISBN: 978-1-914453-20-5
Hardcover ISBN: 978-1-914453-22-9 / 978-1-914453-23-6
Ebook ISBN: 978-1-914453-21-2

Search for 'james shipway guitar' on YouTube and
subscribe for hours of free video lessons!

Join my online community at **totalguitarlab.com** and
get instant access to *all* my premium guitar courses *plus* live training,
workshops and Q&A sessions.

Contents

Introduction

Hello and welcome to *No Bull Barre Chords for Guitar*!

Congratulations on choosing this book; you're about to get a crash course in the essential barre chord shapes that *all* guitarists need.

Many people tell me that they find barre chords tough.

I know what they mean, the first time I tried to play a barre chord I thought my hand was going to explode. I couldn't see how I'd *ever* be able to get my fingers to make the right shape, let alone get a decent sound out of it!

Of course, with practice and perseverance I *did* learn to play them and soon, with what I'll show you in this book, you will too.

You see, I've helped hundreds of guitarists and singer-songwriters learn to use barre chords in the music they play and I've learned a few 'secrets' along the way which can make a big difference - and I'm going to show them to you.

This book will help you:

- Avoid the common problems and mistakes many players make when it comes to learning and playing barre chords
- Learn the most important shapes quickly (*and* get them sounding good!)
- Understand 100% *how* barre chords work so you can get maximum benefit from knowing them
- Learn to use barre chords easily in your playing (*without* it taking years!)
- Be able to play the thousands and thousands of songs which you need barre chords to play, as well as use them to write music of your own

If this all sounds good to you, then great, you're in the right place!

How Should You Use This Book?

For *amazing* results with **No Bull Barre Chords for Guitar** I'd suggest following these **5** simple tips:

1. Start at the beginning and go through the chapters in order!

Even if you have some experience with barre chords already, start at the beginning.

The first few chapters teach you the *essentials* you need for barre chord mastery! You'll learn how barre chords work, how to get them *sounding perfect*, how to avoid the critical errors most players make and lots more...

These early chapters lay the foundation for mastering this skill, so whatever you do, don't skip 'em, even if you *think* you already know what they're going to teach you!

2. Do the practical exercises

Playing and using barre chords is a skill which we master through practice, so, obvious though it may sound, make sure to use the practical exercises I give you.

These are the same kinds of exercises I've used to help *hundreds* of guitar players conquer barre chords. They're short, easy to learn and most importantly, they really work.

All the exercises are written out using guitar fretboard diagrams or simple chord symbols which are easy to understand. There is absolutely no need for you to be able to read written music!

3. Test yourself using the quizzes

Use the quick quiz at the end of some of the chapters to check you've understood everything. The chapters build on each other, so it's important to grasp each one before you progress to the next.

You'll find the answers to the quiz questions too so that you can see how you did.

4. Use the goal tracking checklist for each chapter

At the start of each chapter, we'll be setting some goals for you to shoot for. These tell you what you will have achieved by the end of it.

To help you reach and track these goals, at the end of each chapter you'll find a goal tracking checklist.

Use this to mark off each of these goals as you hit them... a cool way to review your progress, check you know everything you need to know and be 100% certain that you're ready to move on to the next chapter!

5. Don't avoid barre chords ... use them!

Look for opportunities to use barre chords in any music you play. *Integrate them into your playing*. Many people avoid using them because they find them difficult to play. The consequence of this is that they never truly master them!

No matter how tricky they are at first, begin to work barre chords into your playing as soon as possible, and *don't* avoid them. Who cares if they're difficult or don't sound perfect to start with? It's only by using them that they'll get easier and start sounding exactly the way you want them to.

Also, look for barre chords being used in any songs you learn by other people. You'll find them all over the place, they are used a lot! Analyse *why and how* the barre chord shape is being used the way it is. This will massively reinforce your understanding.

If you do this, you'll be well on your way to barre chord success in a *fraction* of the time it takes most other players!

BONUS TIP: Use the FREE Downloadable Practice Tracks!

To help you get even better results with **No Bull Barre Chords for Guitar** I've created some free play-a-long practice tracks.

These give you the opportunity to play the barre chord exercises along with me, just as if we were having a private guitar lesson together!

These are an extremely powerful practice aid so download them and have them at the ready.

To get your optional practice tracks go here:

jamesshipwayguitar.com/barre-chords-audio

By now I'm hoping you're itching to grab your guitar and dive into Chapter 1!

But before you do, I just want to give you a simple explanation of what barre chords are and why they are such powerful tools for guitar players.

It's important to understand this before you begin.

Barre Chords: what are they and why you need 'em!

Barre chords are **movable chord shapes** which can be played *anywhere* on the guitar fingerboard.

They're one of the most powerful and efficient chord playing tools we have as guitar players.

You see, with just a handful of barre chord shapes you can play *hundreds* of chords, without having to learn and memorise *hundreds* of different chord shapes.

For example, with just *one* barre chord shape you can play *every* major chord there is... and with just a simple tweak, you can use the same shape to play *every* minor chord there is and every 7 chord there is.

Pretty cool huh?

Also, with barre chords you can play chords which you simply can't play if you only know the basic open chord shapes that most players start off with.

So, a good working knowledge of barre chords will massively expand your chord vocabulary, make it possible for you to play loads of new songs and pieces of music *and* end those embarrassing or annoying situations when you don't know a shape for the chord you need to play!

Here's the Lowdown on How Barre Chords Work

Let's take a quick look at how you can use barre chords. Don't worry too much about the shapes I'm using here or whether you can play them yet, we'll be covering all of this in detail very soon.

Imagine you wanted to play a G chord and then an A chord:

|G / / / | A / / / / |

There are a few options about which chord shapes to use.

One option would be to use open chords. You'd stay in the same area of the fretboard and use this chord shape for G:

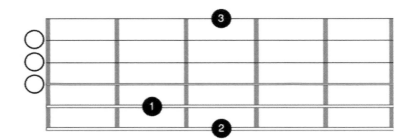

When it was time to play A, you would need to change the chord shape to this A chord shape:

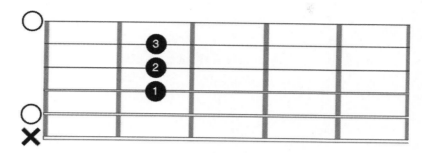

This will work fine, but another option would be to use a barre chord shape. This way you could use the *same* chord shape to play *both* chords. You'd just play it at a *different place* on the guitar neck for each chord. For example, you could use this barre chord shape at the 3rd fret to play G:

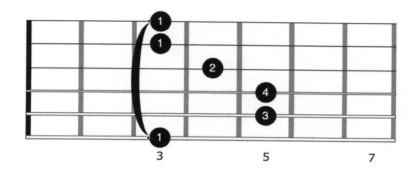

To change to A, you can keep the shape exactly the same. All you need to do is move it up two frets to the 5th fret:

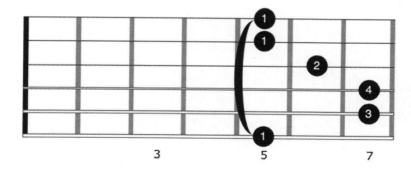

Notice how logical and economical the second approach is!

This is one of the big advantages of being able to use barre chords fluently.

Now, don't worry too much about *why* these chords become G and A when they're moved to these frets, or whether you can actually play these barre chord shapes yet!

I'll be showing you *everything* you need to know very soon, just understand the idea that with barre chords, *one* chord shape can be moved to *different places on the neck* and used to play *many different chords*.

This is why becoming fluent with barre chords is such a transformational step forward for any guitar player: it can quite literally 10x the size of your chord vocabulary!

Let's Get Started!

Ok, I think that's all you need to know about barre chords before you begin, so grab your guitar and let's get started on the road to barre chord mastery.

Good luck, dig in and enjoy!

James

Chapter 1: E Shape Barre Chords

Welcome to Chapter 1!

By the end of this chapter, you will have achieved the following barre chord goals:

1. You will know how to play the 'E shape' barre chord

2. You will know how to use it to play *any* major chord

3. You'll have playing and hand position tips up your sleeve (to get your barre chords sounding *perfect!)*

4. You will be able to *easily* adapt the major shape to get *any* minor chord or any 7 chord you need

5. You will be able to use the 'root note' concept and barre chord shapes to play 36 possible chords!

So, let's dive into it!

Introducing the 'E Shape' Barre Chord

The first barre chord shape we're going to learn is the 'E shape' barre chord.

Not only do we use this chord shape extensively in our playing, but understanding how it works will help you master all the other barre chords as well! This is because all barre chords essentially work in the same way.

This first barre chord shape will also help you build up the strength you need in your fretting hand to get all other barre chords sounding good.

So, getting to grips with this one is an important first step!

The Major Shape

Let's look at how you play a **major** chord using an E shape barre chord. 'Major' is a type of chord, like G major, E major, C major and so on. Most of the time we shorten the name to just the letter name, in other words G major is often referred to as simply 'G'. So, when you hear people talk about chords with names like 'C', 'F' or 'A', they're talking about major chords.

Here's the barre chord shape you need to play a major chord:

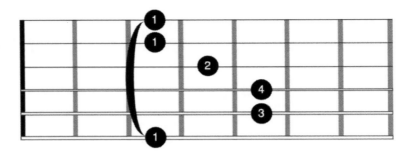

You can start by playing this anywhere on the guitar neck. Try around the 5th or 7th fret, it's easier there than lower down the neck.

If this barre chord shape feels difficult, don't worry because in a moment I'll be giving you some tips to make it easier.

Let's look at where this chord shape actually comes from. You're hopefully familiar with this open chord shape we use to play E major:

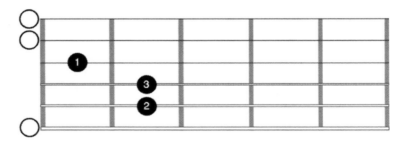

We can move this E chord shape up the neck and use it to play other chords, but we have to move the open strings up as well.

Play the open E major chord again, but this time use your 2nd, 3rd and 4th fingers as shown on the following chord diagram:

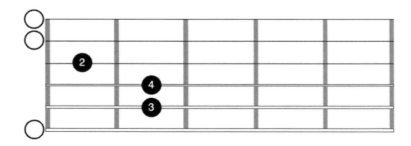

Now, let's suppose we wanted to slide this shape up 1 fret. All the open strings need to move up 1 fret as well. The only finger we have left to play them with is our 1st finger, so we flatten this down across all the open strings in order to play them at the 1st fret. The resulting shape looks like this:

You probably recognise this as the barre chord shape I showed you earlier in this chapter. Well, now you know it is the result of moving the open E major chord (including the open strings) up 1 fret and when we 'flatten' a finger across multiple strings we are making what is called a 'barre'.

So, you can see why the shape is called the 'E shape barre chord'; it's derived from the E chord shape and contains a barre.

Make sense?

Let's Memorise the Major Chord Shape

We're going to learn the chord shape using a method I call the *'Throwing Away'* exercise. I've been using this for years in my guitar lessons and it's a highly effective way of *quickly* learning a new chord shape *and* getting it to stick in your memory.

As we do this exercise, don't worry too much about what the chord *sounds* like. Barre chords take practice and strength to get sounding crisp and clear and you're unlikely to get them sounding perfect straight away!

If your chord sounds scratchy or muted, or if you're hardly getting any sound out of it at all, you can *still* learn the shape thoroughly, so don't let the sound hold you up. Soon we'll look at some things you can do to improve the sound of the chord should you need to.

Here's how to use the *'Throwing Away'* exercise to learn the barre chord shape:

1. Make the chord shape on the neck wherever it feels comfortable (around the 5th fret as before is a good starting point)

2. Now look at the chord. Notice the shape it makes on the guitar neck. Try to take a 'snapshot' in your mind of what the chord looks like

3. Now 'throw away' the chord shape! By 'throw away', what I mean is, take it right off the guitar neck

4. Next, look at the guitar neck and try to 'see' the chord shape on there. Visualise the shape on the strings using the 'snapshot' you took a moment ago

5. When you can see the chord shape, put it back on again

6. Repeat 5-8 times

Put the book down and try this now. Don't rush it, take your time *visualising* the chord shape on the neck (this is the really important part).

I wouldn't be surprised if you find the new shape beginning to stick in your memory quicker than you might have expected it too!

Remember the '***Throwing Away***' exercise, we'll be using it to learn other chord shapes in this book. In fact, it's a *great* way to learn any new chord shape you come across in the future.

Tips for Perfect Barre Chords (and Mistakes to Avoid!)

If you're getting frustrated with how your barre chord shape sounds, then don't! It takes a little time to build up the strength and flexibility you need in your chord hand to get barre chords sounding perfect. Remember, you're asking your hand to do a pretty weird thing and it will take a while before it feels natural.

But there are some common mistakes people make when it comes to playing barre chords, and if you can avoid these then you'll get them sounding perfect much sooner.

Mistake No.1: Bending the Barre!

At first making the barre is tricky! But there are some things you want to avoid so that you train your finger to barre in the *right* way.

Avoid letting the barre bend underneath the guitar neck like in the following photo:

DO NOT: Bend your finger under the neck

Avoid bending your knuckle so the barre lifts away from the fingerboard as in this next photo:

DO NOT: Bend your knuckle

Avoid placing the barre too high up beyond the low strings as shown in the following photo:

DO NOT: Place the barre too high up

Ok, so now you know what *not* to do, let's look at the right way to do it! Study the next picture:

This is the right way!

You can see the 1st finger is 'locked' and *straight*, instead of bending at any point and it extends down *below* the neck instead of curling under it.

It's fine for your finger to be slightly on its side like it is in the following photo. Depending on where on the neck you're playing the barre chord, this may be more comfortable:

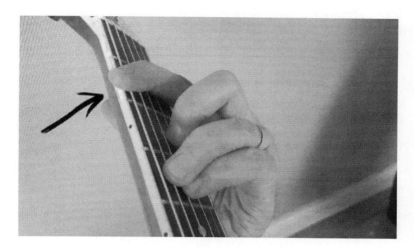

YOU CAN: Put your finger side on

If you're having real problems getting the barre on, think about pushing your wrist 'forward' a little. This can help straighten out the barre and make it easier to get it across the strings. Look at the following photo to see what I mean:

DO: Push your wrist forward

Mistake No.2: Bad Thumb Position!

Thumb position is important because it provides support and gives you something to push the barre against. You basically want to be 'squeezing' the neck between your thumb and the barre, so if your thumb is in the wrong place then this could be tricky.

Avoid putting your thumb over the top of the neck when playing barre chords (see following photo):

DO NOT: Put your thumb over the top

Avoid letting your thumb drop down too low on the back of the neck (see following photo):

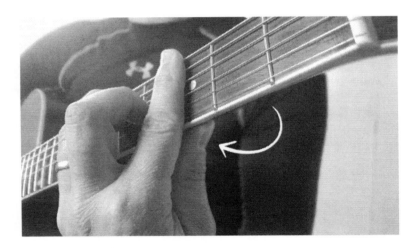

DO NOT: Let your thumb drop low

Avoid letting the thumb go flat on the back of the neck (see following photo):

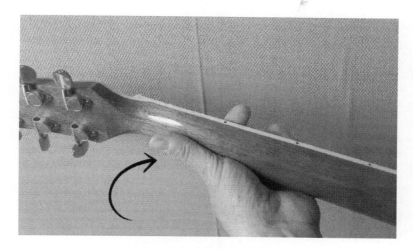

DO NOT: Let your thumb go flat

So where should your thumb go? I suggest putting the thumb behind the neck in a central position. It wants to be roughly level with the barre. This will give the necessary support and stability (see following photo):

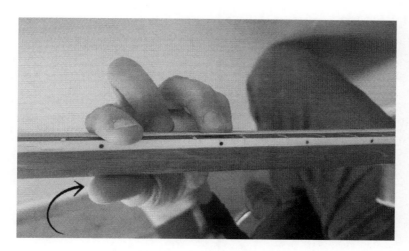

DO: Let your thumb be central on the back of the neck

Push your 'thumbprint' against the neck. This will give you something solid to push the barre against to get it flatter. You can see me doing this in the following picture:

DO: Push your thumbprint against the back of the neck

This will feel like hard work at first and your thumb is going to wonder what is going on! A little regular practice though will soon build up the strength and it will soon start to feel much easier.

Mistake No.3: Collapsing Fingers!

Pressing down the barre is awkward at first and this can cause the other fingers to collapse and stop the notes in the chord ringing clearly. This becomes less of a problem as your hand gets stronger through practice, but try and avoid the following common problems if you can.

Avoid letting your fingers collapse and go flat on the strings, as is happening in the following photo:

DO NOT: Collapse your fingers

Avoid letting your fingers bend backwards (see following photo):

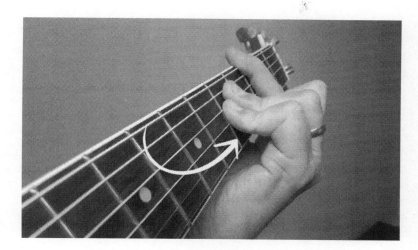

DO NOT: Let your fingers bend backwards

You want to aim to keep your fingers on their tips and pressing 'into' the fingerboard to get a firm contact with the string (see following photo):

DO: Keep your fingers on their tips

Overall, they should look 'tidy', instead of sticking out at all sorts of different angles!

Look at the following photos to see all these factors used together to make for a well played barre chord:

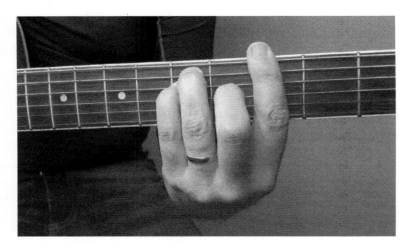

A well played barre chord

A well played barre chord (from a different angle)

You can see the barre is straight and flat, the thumb is behind the neck and the fingers are on their tips. The whole shape looks tidy.

Rest assured, it took a little practice for me to train my fingers to do this, but by knowing what you're aiming for, you can check your hand position and train yourself to do it the right way too.

The Root Note: the Key to Using Barre Chords!

We said earlier that a single barre chord shape can be used to play many different chords. Instead of changing the *shape* to change chord, we simply move the barre chord shape to a *different* place on the guitar neck.

The E shape major barre chord shape you just learned can be used to play *any* major chord you might need to play. You just need to know *where* to move it to, to get a particular chord.

Learning to do this is easy once you know about the *root note*.

What is the Root Note?

The *root note* is the note the chord is built on. For example, in a G chord the root would be the note G. In a D chord the root note would be D. Root notes are the key to being able to use barre chords fluently.

How Root Notes Work

All the barre chord shapes we're going to study contain the *root note*. On many of the chord diagrams used in this book the root note is marked with an 'R' inside a white disc or just with a white disc.

With the E shape barre chord the root note is on the low E string:

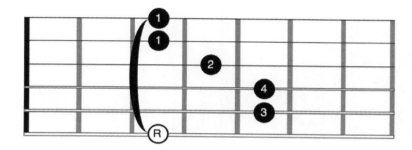

A little knowledge of the low E string will quickly unlock the ability to use this barre chord shape. Here are some of the notes along the low E string:

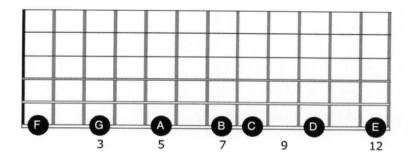

All we need to do is line the root note in the barre chord shape up with the right note on the E string. This will give us the chord we want.

Let's say for example you needed to play a **B** major chord:

1. Find **B** on the low E string (it's at the **7th** fret)
2. Play the chord shape with the barre across the 7th fret

Instant B chord!

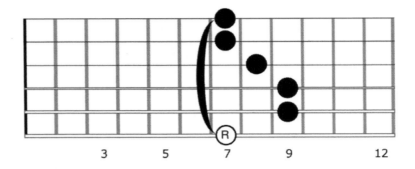

Need an **F** major chord?

1. Find **F** on the low E string (it's at the **1st** fret)
2. Play the chord shape with the barre across the 1st fret

Instant F chord!

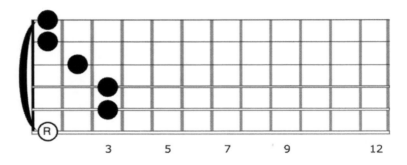

This is basically how the barre chord shape works but that's not all; there are other chords we can play with this powerful shape.

In between the notes shown on the diagram above there are some extra notes. Let's call these the *sharps* and *flats*. The symbol for sharp is **#** and the symbol for flat is **b.** When we add the sharps and flats to the notes we looked at a moment ago we get all of the 12 notes which we use to make music.

For more on this read about **The Musical Alphabet** in my '**No Bull Music Theory for Guitarists***'* book.

Now, we can play the barre chord shape starting on a sharp or flat note as well.

The following image shows all 12 notes along the low E string:

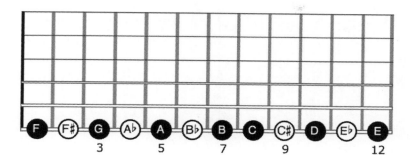

Imagine you needed to play a **Bb** major chord:

1. Find **Bb** on the low E string (it's at the **6th** fret)
2. Play the chord shape with the barre across the 6th fret

Instant Bb chord!

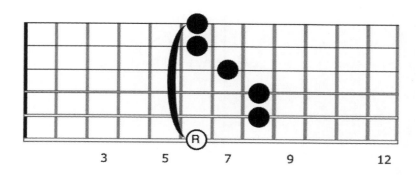

If you wanted to play a **C#** major chord:

1. Find **C#** on the low E string (it's at the **9th** fret)
2. Play the chord shape with the barre across the 9th fret

Instant C# chord!

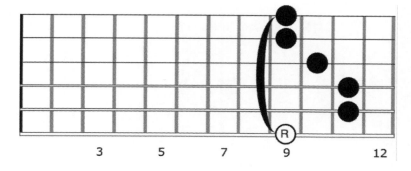

And that is how root notes and barre chord shapes are used together…

There are some practical exercises coming very soon to help you learn and master this, but first, read the above section on root notes as many times as you need to so it makes total sense. It's crucially important! Understanding about root notes *is the key* to becoming awesome at using barre chords in the music you play.

Now, there's a good chance you might be wondering:

How do I know when I should use a barre chord instead of an open chord?

This is a good question. You need to understand that barre chords and open chords are just different *methods* to achieve the *same thing*. It doesn't matter whether we use an open chord shape or a barre chord shape to play a G chord... it's still just a G chord!

You can choose whether to use an open chord shape or a barre shape to play a particular chord. There is a slight difference in the sound, but as long as you're playing the right chord it will make virtually no difference.

Easily Changing the Major Shape into Minor

Now that you can play a major barre chord shape, playing a minor chord is easy! By simply lifting off one finger, the major barre chord shape can be used to play *any* minor chord as well.

It really is as easy as that! Let's look at how this works.

Here's the major chord shape again:

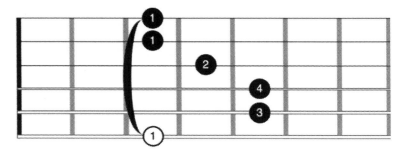

Remove your 2nd finger from the G string and the chord is changed from major to minor:

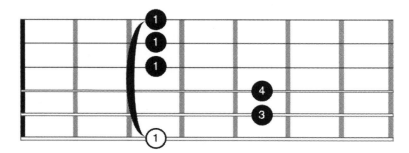

Amazing! You can now use everything you've learned about playing major barre chords to play minor chords as well; you just need to lift off your 2nd finger from the major barre chord shape.

If you needed to play a **G minor** chord:

1. Find **G** on the low E string (it's at the **3rd** fret)
2. Play the minor chord shape (2nd finger off) with the barre across the 3rd fret

Instant G minor chord!

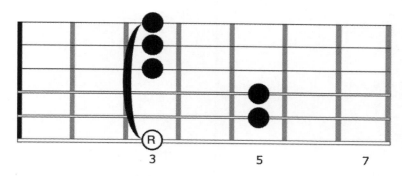

Of course, this works for *sharps* and *flats* as well.

For an **F# minor** chord:

1. Find **F#** on the low E string (it's at the **2nd** fret)
2. Play the minor chord shape (2nd finger off) with the barre across the 2nd fret

Instant F# minor chord!

Now you can use the E shape barre chord to play *any* major chord *and* with just a simple tweak, any minor chord too! That's 24 possible chords in total, with almost a single chord shape.

I'm sure you're starting to see the awesome power of barre chords by now, but it gets even better...

Easily Changing the Major Shape into a Dominant 7 Chord

Another commonly seen chord is the *dominant seven* chord. You've probably played these before, they're normally just written as a '7'. For example, A7, E7, D7 etc.

To get the barre chord shape for playing a 7 chord, simply lift off the 4th (or little) finger from the major shape.

This gives you the following barre chord shape:

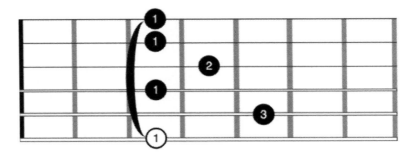

So, if you needed to play a **C7** chord:

1. Find **C** on the low E string (it's at the **8th** fret)
2. Play the 7 chord shape (4th finger off) with the barre across the 8th fret

Instant C7 chord!

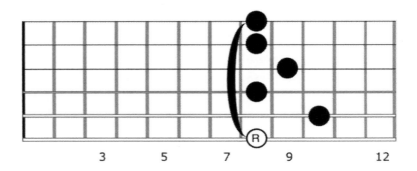

It works for *sharps* and *flats* as well.

For an **Ab7** chord:

1. Find **Ab** on the low E string (it's at the **4th** fret)
2. Play the 7 chord shape (4th finger off) with the barre across the 4th fret

Instant Ab7 chord!

Lots of songs use nothing more complicated than major, minor and 7 chords and now you have a way to play any major, minor or 7 chord there is!

Think how it is going to transform your knowledge of chords and the music you'll be able to play as a result!

Before we move onto some practical exercises to help you apply this knowledge to the guitar, let's summarise what you've learned so far in this chapter:

- You know the **major** shape for playing an **E shape barre chord**
- You know what the **root note** is
- You know how the **chord shape, root note** and the **notes** on the low E string work together to make **any major chord**
- You can **convert** the major chord into a **minor** chord simply by lifting off your 2nd finger
- You can **convert** the major shape into a **7** chord simply by lifting off your 4th finger
- You can see how all this can be used to play *any* **major**, **minor** or **7** chord there is!

Read over any of this material as many times as you need to for it to be 100% clear. Then grab your guitar and move on to the practical exercises coming up next!

Use The Following Practical Exercises to Master This Chapter

How should you practice your barre chords and what should you do to master them?

Well, that's what I've tried to show you below. I've set you **5 simple exercises** to help you to understand, consolidate and apply what you've learned in this chapter.

Follow these simple guidelines as you work through them:

Try to spend **3 to 5 minutes** on **3 exercises** each day you practice. This will only take 10-15 minutes of your time and will quickly pay off. If you can practice every day then you'll see awesome results very quickly. If you can't play daily then you'll still see progress, it may just take a little longer. Just practice as often as you can.

Remember, your barre chords probably won't sound perfect to start with and that's ok! Just make sure to follow the tips on hand position and get them sounding as good as you can. Be patient and give yourself some time to build up your hand strength.

Barre chords are tiring and demanding to begin with so take short 10-20 second breaks as needed during each exercise to prevent fatigue and strain setting in.

Take your time, don't rush. Persevere and be patient - you will be rewarded!

Exercise 1: Throw Away the Shape

1. Make the major barre chord shape at any fret you like
2. Use the '**Throwing Away**' exercise to thoroughly learn it
3. Repeat over and over, periodically moving to a different fret

Exercise 2: Note Finding

Using the fretboard diagram that follows, memorise the notes F, G, A and B along the low E string. If you have dots/fret markers along the neck of your guitar use them to help.

Now learn where to find C, D and E.

Once you know all these notes thoroughly, learn the sharp (#) and flat (*b*) notes too.

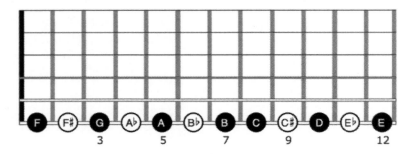

Exercise 3: Make it Minor

1. Play the major barre chord shape at any fret
2. Convert it to a minor chord by lifting off your 2nd finger
3. Move to different frets and repeat

Make sure you know which shape is major and which is minor, don't get them mixed up!

Exercise 4: Major to Minor to 7

1. Play the major barre chord shape at any fret
2. Convert it to a minor chord
3. Turn it back into a major chord
4. Now convert it to a 7 chord by lifting off your 4th finger

Move to different frets and repeat. Make sure you know which shape is major, which is minor and which is 7!

Exercise 5: Chord Finding

Using the major, minor and 7 barre shapes seen so far and your knowledge of the notes on the E string, play the following sequences of chords:

F major to Fm to F7
G major to Gm to G7
A major to Am to A7
B major to Bm to B7
C major to Cm to C7
D major to Dm to D7

Quick Quiz

Test yourself with this quiz, then check how you did using the answers which follow.

Play the following major, minor or 7 chords using the E shape barre chords from this chapter:

F
A7
Gm
C
Dm
B
B*b*7
F#m
A*b*
C#m

Find out how you did!

F (1st fret major shape)
A7 (5th fret 7 shape)
Gm (3rd fret minor shape)
C (8th fret major shape)
Dm (10th fret minor shape)
B (7th fret major shape)
Bb7 (6th fret 7 shape)
F#m (2nd fret minor shape)
Ab (4th fret major shape)
C#m (9th fret minor shape)

Have You Reached Your Goals?

Let's see how you did with the goals we set at the start of this chapter. Check off each one when you're sure you've achieved it.

I can play the 'E shape' major barre chord [   ]

I'm using the playing and hand position tips to play the shape [   ]

I can change the major shape to get a minor chord [   ]

I can change the major shape to get a 7 (dominant 7) chord [   ]

I can use the root note concept to play 36 possible chords [   ]

Checked all the goals off?

Congratulations! You have taken a huge step towards mastering barre chords.

If you need to go back and spend some more time on any part of this chapter then this is what you should do. There's no rush and covering everything thoroughly will help you make faster progress through the rest of this book.

When you're ready, move on to the next chapter where we're going to look at powerful exercises to get you totally comfortable at actually *using* these E shape barre chords in the music you play.

We'll look at switching between barre chords, changing into barre chords from open chords and lots more.

See you there!

Chapter 2: E Shape Barre Chord Training

Welcome to Chapter 2!

The first chapter was all about learning the E barre chord shapes and gaining an understanding about how they work.

This is a crucial first step, but to use barre chord shapes fluently we need to go beyond that. We must be able to smoothly connect them up on the guitar neck to play sequences of different chords. We must also learn to combine them with other types of chord shape, like basic open chords. Then we'll be able to actually *use* barre chords when we play the music of our choice.

How can you learn to do this? Simply by following the **3 Step Plan** in this chapter! This will help you achieve the following barre chord goals:

1. You'll become fluent at moving E shape barre chords around the neck

2. You'll be able to switch between major, minor and 7 chords using the E shape barre chord

3. You'll be able to change between barre chords and various open chord shapes (and use them together in any songs you like to play)

4. You will be able to apply strumming patterns whilst changing between multiple chords (open and barre shapes)

So, grab your guitar and let's begin!

The '3 Golden Rules' For Perfect Chord Changing

Before we begin, I want to mention three powerful principles or 'rules' to follow when learning to switch between chord shapes. Use these when learning to change between *any* set of chord shapes, not just with barre chords.

Rule 1: Know The Chord Shapes... *Thoroughly!*

Make sure you are 100% *certain* about the chord shapes you are using *before* you even try changing between them. This means knowing *exactly* where your fingers need to go to play them, without any hesitation or guesswork! This may sound obvious, but you'd be amazed how many guitarists struggle switching between chords simply because they don't know the shapes well enough. Nailing the chord shapes first makes switching between them a *whole* lot easier.

Rule 2: See Where You're Going... *Before* it's Time to Move!

Get into the habit of visualising the chord shape you are moving to on the guitar neck *before* it's time to change to it. Try to clearly 'see' it on the fingerboard. This prepares you for the chord change, making a good change much easier to achieve. When it's time to change to the new chord, you've already worked out where you need to move to, you just need to get your fingers there.

Rule 3: Only Move the Fingers That *Need* To Move!

Sometimes a finger is in the same place for two different chord shapes. Look at the following chord shape for an open position C chord:

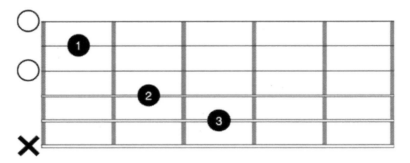

Now look at this F barre chord shape:

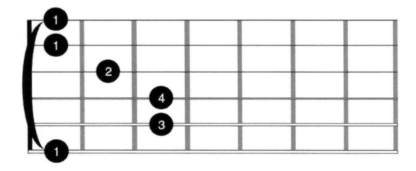

You can see that the 3rd finger is in exactly the same place for both shapes, on the A string at the 3rd fret. So, if we are changing from C to F we don't need to move this finger at all. Keeping a finger anchored in this way makes the change a lot easier because there is less to do.

Look out for this shortcut in any chord changes you encounter, it can help you get faster, smoother, more accurate chord changes.

Remember these **3 Golden Rules** as you go through the rest of this book. They may seem obvious, but they will really speed up your progress!

The 3 Step Plan for Mastering E Shape Barre Chords

By using this **3 Step Plan** you can soon become fluent at using the E shape barre chords in your playing. Go through the steps in order using the exercises and guidelines given and with as little as 10-15 minutes practice each day you can conquer these barre chords in a *fraction* of the time it takes most players.

Practice, repetition and perseverance are the key things here, so stick with it and you can be sure that you'll see great results. Let's go!

Step 1: Moving the Same Barre Chord

The easiest way to start is to get used to moving the exact same barre chord shape around. We'll start with the major shape before moving on to the minor and dominant 7 shapes.

Moving the Major Chord Shape

Let's use the major barre chord shape to play a G chord at the 3rd fret:

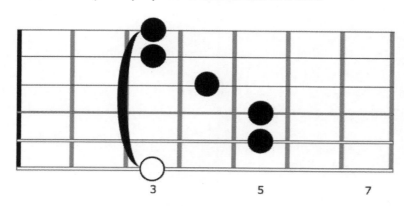

Now use the same shape to play A at the 5th fret:

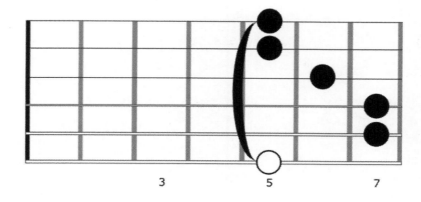

Now let's practice switching between them.

Here's the best way to do this:

1. Play the G chord at the 3rd fret
2. Now look ahead and 'see' the A chord at the 5th fret
3. Relax the G chord so you're not pressing down but *leave your fingers in the shape of the chord* (this is important!)
4. Now the chord shape is relaxed, it can be moved. Gently shift it up to the 5th fret trying to maintain the chord shape with your fingers
5. Now press it down again to get the A chord
6. Now follow the exact same process to change back down to G again

Repeat this exercise 5-6 times, taking short breaks if your hand becomes tired.

Notice how we *continue making* the barre chord shape with our fingers as we move. This is very important. We want to shift the *whole shape*, not move to a new fret and then rebuild it again. Your fingers may not like this at first and the shape may crumble as you move it. This is totally normal! Just persevere, keep your hand as relaxed as you can, focus on maintaining the shape as best you can and you'll quickly see this habit begin to form.

You'll also notice that we are not trying to keep a rhythmic strumming pattern going as we change chords. This is because we need to train our fingers to move from chord to chord smoothly *without* the distraction of doing anything else at the same time. Many guitarists have big problems switching between chords at first because they're trying to juggle too many new things at once! Get the chord change good and only then add strumming. Doing this makes the whole learning process much easier and much less frustrating!

Now, using the guidelines given a moment ago practice changing between the following pairs of major chords using the major barre chord shape:

F (1st fret) to **G** (3rd fret)
A (5th fret) to **B** (7th fret)
B (7th fret) to **C** (8th fret)

Remember to 'look ahead' for the shape you are moving to and keep the chord shape relaxed but intact as you shift it. The importance of this can't be overemphasized.

Also make sure that you're playing the barre chord the best you can each time. Don't let moving the shape around cause the barre to bend under the neck, or your fingers to collapse, or any of the other mistakes we talked about earlier creep in!

Moving the Minor Chord Shape

Now let's practice moving some minor chords around.

Play Gm at the 3rd fret:

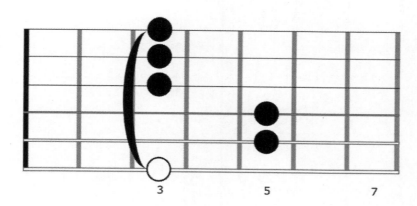

Practice shifting this shape up to the 5th fret to get Am:

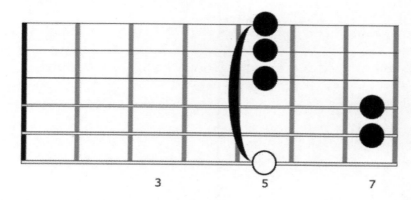

Keep looking ahead for the chord you are changing to and maintain the chord shape with your fingers as you shift it. Relax your hand and just let the chord shape glide along the strings to the new fret.

Now practice changing between these pairs of minor chords using the minor barre chord shape:

Fm (1st fret) to **Gm** (3rd fret)
Am (5th fret) to **Bm** (7th fret)
Bm (7th fret) to **Cm** (8th fret)

Moving the 7 Chord Shape

Next, we'll practice moving dominant 7 chords around.

Play G7 at the 3rd fret:

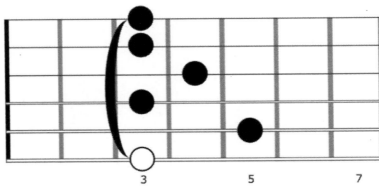

Practice shifting this shape up to the 5th fret to get A7:

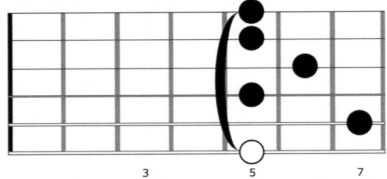

As you do this, follow all the guidelines covered so far (you know them by now!).

Now practice changing between these pairs of 7 chords using the dominant 7 barre chord shape:

F7 (1st fret) to **G7** (3rd fret)
A7 (5th fret) to **B7** (7th fret)
B7 (7th fret) to **C7** (8th fret)

Spend as long as you need to on these exercises to get comfortable with them and don't worry if you find moving barre chords tough at first, it's like that for everyone! Just patiently do the exercises, go at your own pace and you'll start to see and feel it getting easier.

How To Become Awesome at Strumming and Changing Chords (Together!)

It's best to train your chord hand to switch between shapes *without* trying to keep a strumming rhythm going at the same time, but it can make the exercises seem a bit mechanical and unmusical as you practice them.

So, once you are changing between a pair of chords easily and smoothly, it's okay to add in some strumming.

Many guitarists struggle and become discouraged when it comes to changing chords and strumming at the same time. They feel like there is just too much to do at once! So here are three powerful rules which will make sure you avoid the trouble so many players experience:

Rule 1: The Strumming Hand Does *Not* Wait For the Chord Changing Hand!

I've taught thousands of guitar lessons on chord changing and strumming and this is the number one mistake people make. Do *not* break your strumming whilst you change to the new chord, keep the strumming going no matter what!

Your chord changing hand must learn to keep up with the strumming hand. The best way to train it to do this is to keep strumming *even* if you haven't got the new chord shape in place yet. The strumming hand must *not* wait for the chord to be ready.

Now, this may sound a little crazy. I mean, why would you want to strum a chord shape which wasn't in place yet?

It's because if you don't do it this way, your chord hand becomes really good at holding the strumming hand up! This makes it almost impossible to play anything musical because you can't keep any rhythm going. Keeping the strumming going when you change to a different chord shape forces your chord hand to get its act together (and it will, quite quickly).

Now, to start with you're probably going to have a few clunky sounding chords when your fingers are late getting to the chord shape. Don't worry about this, it's totally normal. Just follow this rule and you will be amazed at how quickly both hands begin to work together to produce smooth, rhythmic sounding chord changes.

Rule 2: Keep It Simple!

Start with basic strumming rhythms which are easy for you to play. Then you can focus on strumming and getting a good chord change instead of getting tangled up in a difficult strumming pattern.

Master the basics in this way and soon you'll be able to change chords and do all sorts of fancy strumming patterns at the same time without having any problems.

Not sure how to start applying strumming to chord changing?

Try taking any of the two chord exercises we've seen so far in this chapter. Let's start with a G chord at the 3rd fret moving to A at the 5th fret. We'll play each chord for 2 bars:

|G / / / | G / / / | A / / / | A / / / |

There are normally 4 beats in a bar of music. In the previous example, the chord name represents one beat and the three 'slashes' (/) represent the remaining three beats.

|G/// |G/// |A/// |A///|
  1 234   1 234   1 234   1 234

I'd suggest strumming once on each beat to begin with. This means you'll be strumming 4 times in each bar.

This is a very simple strumming pattern but it's a good place to start. As you get used to strumming whilst changing chords you can add in some more strums to make it more interesting if you want to. Experiment, just make sure your strumming sounds rhythmic and in time.

Rule 3: Keep It Slow!

You'll develop this skill quicker if you practice it slowly to begin with. Many players rush, make mistakes and get frustrated when all they need to do is slow the exercise down to make it easier to play.

Try to avoid the temptation to rush. Go as slowly as you need to in order to make the exercise easy for you.

In summary, as you go through the remainder of this chapter, complete each chord changing exercise *without* any rhythmic strumming to begin with. Once the exercise feels easier, feel free to incorporate any strumming rhythms you want (but make sure you're following the guidelines I just outlined!).

Step 2: Moving Between Different Shapes

Once you're comfortable moving the same barre chord shape around, it's time to start mixing up the major, minor and dominant 7 shapes.

Changing Between Major and Minor

Let's use the major barre chord shape to play a G chord at the 3rd fret:

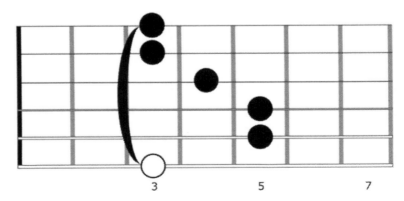

Now use the minor barre shape to play Am at the 5th fret:

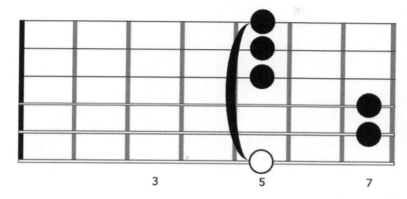

Practice switching between these 5-6 times. Look ahead, maintain the chord shape with your fingers and follow all the other guidelines we talked about earlier.

Changing Between Major and 7

Let's use the major barre chord shape to play an F chord at the 1st fret:

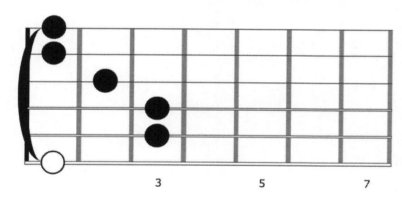

Now use the 7 barre shape to play G7 at the 3rd fret:

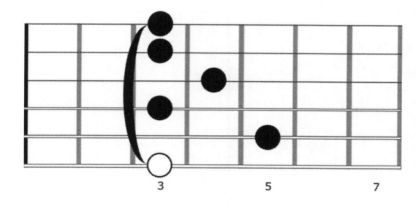

Practice switching slowly and accurately between these 5-6 times.

Changing Between Minor and 7

Use the minor barre chord shape to play an Am chord at the 5th fret:

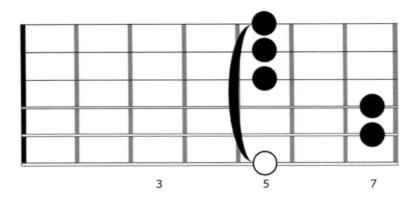

Now use the 7 barre shape to play G7 at the 3rd fret:

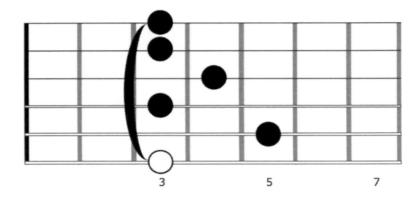

Practice switching between Am and G7. Do this 5-6 times.

Combining All 3 Shapes!

You can practice the following set of exercises along to the free audio tracks which come with this book – go here to get them: **jamesshipwayguitar.com/barre-chords-audio**

Now let's have a go at mixing up all the barre chord shapes we've covered so far. From now on I won't be telling you what fret to move the shapes to, I'll be leaving this part to you. This will help you become an expert at learning how to use these barre chord shapes.

To begin, try changing from Am to G to F to G7 with one bar on each chord:

| Am / / / | G / / / | F / / / | G7 / / / |  **Audio Track 2.1**

Remember to slowly practice switching from shape to shape, looking ahead as you go and maintaining as much of the barre chord shape as you can when you change to the next chord.

Then, only when you feel ready, add in some simple strumming. If you're an experienced strummer then just go with what feels comfortable and sounds good to you. If strumming is new to you then start very simply by just strumming once on each beat (4 strums on each chord).

When the exercise feels easy loop it round and round as if you were playing a song using these chords.

Here are some more great exercises for learning to mix up different chords. Go through these at your own pace in the same way you did with the previous exercise. For now, play each chord only with the major, minor or 7 variation of the E shape barre chord and add in strumming only when you've got the chord changing sounding good.

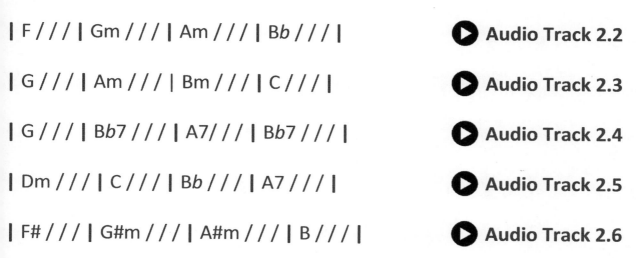

| F / / / | Gm / / / | Am / / / | B♭ / / / | ▶ **Audio Track 2.2**

| G / / / | Am / / / | Bm / / / | C / / / | ▶ **Audio Track 2.3**

| G / / / | B♭7 / / / | A7/ / / | B♭7 / / / | ▶ **Audio Track 2.4**

| Dm / / / | C / / / | B♭ / / / | A7 / / / | ▶ **Audio Track 2.5**

| F# / / / | G#m / / / | A#m / / / | B / / / | ▶ **Audio Track 2.6**

When you can play each of these exercises you will have made a huge breakthrough with your barre chords! So, take your time and follow all the guidelines given as you work on each one.

When you're ready move onto Step 3.

Step 3: Combining Barre Chords and Open Chords

In a lot of situations you'll want to combine the big, resonant sound of open chords, with the portability and flexibility of barre chords. Learning to do this is the focus of this final step.

Changing from an open chord to a barre chord (or vice-versa) normally requires a little more work from our chord hand than moving the same barre chord shape around the neck does, but once you're happy with using barre chord shapes, most chord changes are pretty easy.

Work through the exercises that follow to become fluent at combining open chords and barre chords. Remember to start slow, look ahead to see where you're moving your fingers to, and watch for any fingers which are in the same place for both shapes and can be left down. Add strumming *only* when the chord changes are smooth!

(**Note**: If you're unsure of the shapes for any of the open chords here, see the *Useful Open Chord Shapes* section at the back of this book).

Two Chord Changes

Let's start by changing between just two chords. Practice the basic chord changing move first. Then when you're ready, play 2 bars on each chord and loop the resulting 4 bar chord sequence round and round.

When you become awesome at this, try just playing 1 bar on each chord then change to the next one.

Use the following exercises:

C (open chord shape) to **F** (barre shape)

| : C / / / | C / / / | F / / / | F / / / : | ▶ **Audio Track 2.7**

Am (open chord shape) to **F** (barre shape)

| : Am / / / | Am / / / | F / / / | F / / / : | ▶ **Audio Track 2.8**

G (open chord shape) to **F** (barre shape)

| : G / / / | G / / / | F / / / | F / / / : | ▶ **Audio Track 2.9**

E (open chord shape) to **F#m** (barre shape)

| : E / / / | E / / / | F#m / / / | F#m / / / : | ▶ **Audio Track 2.10**

D (open chord shape) to **F#m** (barre shape)

| : D / / / | D / / / | F#m / / / | F#m / / / : | ▶ **Audio Track 2.11**

C (open chord shape) to **G7** (barre shape)

| : C / / / | C / / / | G7 / / / | G7 / / / : | ▶ **Audio Track 2.12**

G (barre shape) to **Em** (open chord shape)

|: G / / / | G / / / | Em / / / | Em / / / :|

▶ **Audio Track 2.13**

Gm (barre shape) to **D7** (open chord shape)

|: Gm / / / | Gm / / / | D7 / / / | D7 / / / :|

▶ **Audio Track 2.14**

Got the hang of these? Let's move on!

More Complex Chord Sequences

Now apply all the same practice techniques and methods you used on the two chord exercises to the more complex examples below. These are all common chord sequences, you may even recognise some from songs you know!

C (open) **Am** (open) **G7** (barre) **F** (barre)

|: C / / / | Am / / / | G7 / / / | F / / / :|

▶ **Audio Track 2.15**

C (open) **Dm** (open) **Em** (open) **F** (barre)

|: C / / / | Dm / / / | Em / / / | F / / / :|

▶ **Audio Track 2.16**

A (open) **E** (open) **F#m** (barre) **D** (open)

|: A / / / | E / / / | F#m / / / | D / / / :|

▶ **Audio Track 2.17**

D (open) **F#m** (barre) **G** (barre) **A7** (barre)

|: D / / / | F#m / / / | G / / / | A7 / / / :|

▶ **Audio Track 2.18**

D (open) **A** (open) **F#m** (barre) **G** (barre)

|: D / / / | A / / / | F#m / / / | G / / / :|

▶ **Audio Track 2.19**

E (open) **G#m** (barre) **A** (barre) **Am** (barre)

|: E / / / | G#m / / / | A / / / | Am / / / :|  **Audio Track 2.20**

Have You Reached Your Goals?

If you can fluently play through all the examples in this chapter, then congratulations! You've taken a huge step forward in your quest to master using barre chords in your guitar playing.

If you ever tried playing a song which used some barre chords but abandoned it because it was just too difficult... return to it and see if it is now easier. I'll bet it will be!

Let's see how you did with the goals we set at the start of this chapter. Check off each one when you're confident you've achieved it.

I am fluent at moving E shape barre chords around the neck   [   ]

I can switch between major, minor and 7 chords using the E shape barre chord   [   ]

I can change between barre chords and various open chord shapes (and use them together to play chord sequences)   [   ]

I can apply strumming patterns whilst changing between multiple chords (both open shapes and barre shapes)   [   ]

Checked all the goals off?

Awesome, well done!

Then it's time to move on to the next chapter where we'll look at another essential barre chord: the A shape barre chord. With E *and* A shape barre chords, you'll have nearly everything you need to become ultra fluent at using barre chords to play *most* music. Even better, the A shape barre chords will be easier to learn and play now that you're an expert when it comes to the E shape chords.

So, when you're ready, grab your guitar and I'll see you in Chapter 3!

Chapter 3: A Shape Barre Chords

Welcome to Chapter 3!

By the end of this chapter, you will have achieved the following barre chord goals:

1. You will know how to play the 'A shape' major barre chord

2. You will know how to use it to play *any* major chord

3. You will know how to play the 'A shape' minor barre chord

4. You will know how to play the 'A shape' dominant 7 barre chord

5. You will be able to use the notes on the A string and the A shape barre chords to play 36 *more* chords!

So, let's get started!

Introducing the 'A Shape' Barre Chord

It's time to add another barre chord shape into your arsenal: the 'A shape' barre chord. When you can use this alongside the E shape chord, you'll have most of the barre chord knowledge you need!

The Major Shape

Here's how you play a **major** chord using an A shape barre chord:

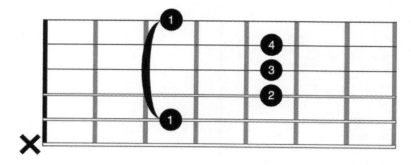

The finger position I've shown you in the previous diagram is the most common way to play this chord and if it works for you, use it. However, some people (like me) find it a little awkward. Normally I prefer to barre across the D, G and B strings with my 3rd finger like this:

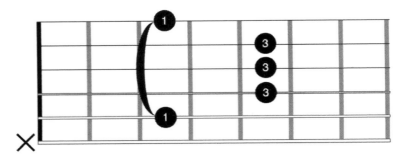

Or, I'll barre across the D, G and B strings with my 4th finger:

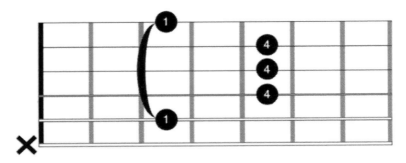

So which fingering should you use? There are advantages and disadvantages to all three of these approaches and I'd suggest going with the one that feels easiest for now. You can always change later if you decide to.

If, instead of using all four fingers, you decide to barre with your 3rd or 4th finger then you'll need to try and bend your finger at the knuckle as shown in the following photos:

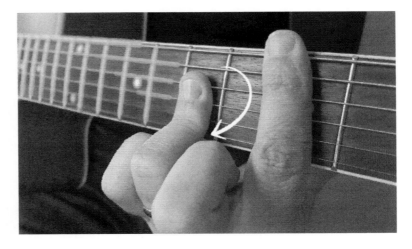

Barre with 3rd finger

Barre with 4th finger

If you don't do this you will likely barre across the top E string as well and the chord won't sound right. Although this takes a little practice, it's necessary if you choose to play the chord this way.

Start by playing this shape around the 3rd or 5th fret, it's easier there than lower down the neck.

Just as with the E shape chord, this barre chord shape is derived from a familiar open chord shape, in this case A:

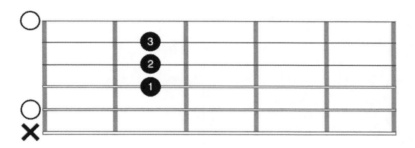

When we move this shape (including the open strings) up the neck, the result is the A shape major barre chord we've just seen. Because the open A chord does not include the open low E string, this string is *not* included in the barre chord shape either. So, remember, A shape barre chords are only played across five strings, the low E string is left out.

Let's Memorise the Major Chord Shape

You've probably already built up some strength in your hand from working on the E shape barre chord and may find the A shape chord easier than the E shape chord did to begin with. If so, then great!

Even if it doesn't sound perfect right now, you can still memorise the chord shape thoroughly. Persevere, experiment to find which of the fingerings you prefer and in time you'll have it sounding great.

So, let's use the '**Throwing Away**' exercise to learn the A shape major barre chord now.

1. Make the chord shape on the neck wherever it feels comfortable (around the 3rd-5th fret as before is a good starting point)
2. Now look at the chord and take a 'snapshot' in your mind of what it looks like
3. Now 'throw away' the chord shape (drop your fingers off the strings)
4. Look back at the guitar neck and visualise the shape on the strings using the 'snapshot' you took a moment ago
5. When you can 'see' the chord shape, put it back on again
6. Repeat 5-8 times

Make sure you put this book down and do the exercise and remember to take your time to clearly *visualise* the chord shape on the neck, this step is vital.

Quick Reminder: Mistakes to Avoid!

As you practice this new barre chord shape, remember to watch out for and avoid the barre chord mistakes we discussed earlier.

Try to make sure:

- The barre is not bending, lifting up, or 'curling' under the neck
- Your thumb is in a solid supporting position behind the neck so that you can press the barre against it
- Your other fingers are on their tips as much as possible (unless of course you are making a barre with your 3rd or 4th finger)

Just like with the E shape chord it may take a while before this chord feels natural and easy to play – but keep working at it!

The A String Root Note

Earlier in this book we talked about the *root note*. We saw how we can line the root note in the E shape barre chord up with the notes on the low E string to get any major, minor or dominant 7 chord.

The A shape barre chords work in *exactly* the same way with one important difference: the root note is now on the A string.

Here are the notes along the A string without the sharps and flats:

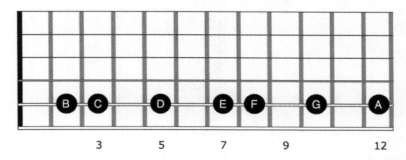

Now we can match up the root note in the shape with the notes on the A string to get any major chord we want to play.

Say for example you needed to play a **C** major chord:

- Find **C** on the low A string (it's at the **3rd** fret)
- Play the chord shape with the barre across the 3rd fret (remembering to miss out the low E string)

Instant C chord!

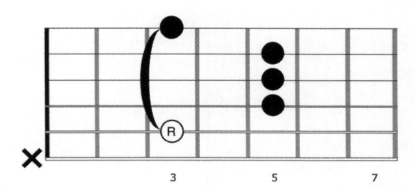

Need an **F** major chord?

- Find **F** on the low A string. It's at the **8th** fret
- Play the chord shape with the barre across the 8th fret

Instant F chord!

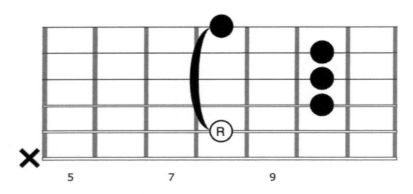

Of course, we can play the barre chord shape starting on a sharp or flat note as well. Here are all 12 notes shown along the low A string:

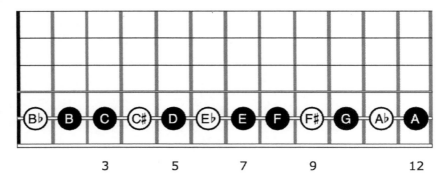

Let's imagine you needed to play an **Eb** major chord:

- Find **Eb** on the A string (it's at the **6th** fret)
- Play the chord shape with the barre across the 6th fret

Instant E♭ chord!

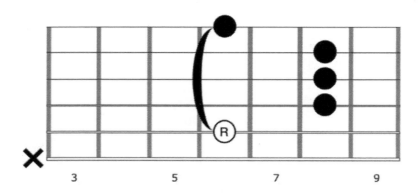

If you wanted to play an **F#** major chord:

- Find **F#** on the A string (find it at the **9th** fret)
- Play the chord shape with the barre across the 9th fret

Instant F# chord!

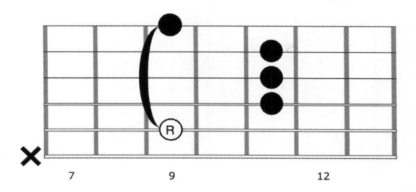

There are some practical exercises coming soon to help you become fluent at moving the A shape barre chord around to get any chord you want. But first, let's look at minor and dominant 7 chords.

Changing the Major Shape into Minor

The major shape can be changed and used to play minor chords. We just need to alter the arrangement of our fingers as shown on the following diagram:

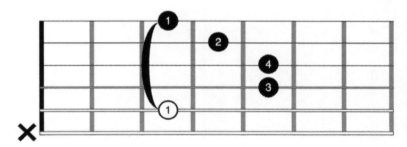

You can now use this shape and the notes along the A string to play any minor chord you want to play.

If you needed to play a **B minor** chord:

- Find **B** on the A string (it's at the **2nd** fret)
- Play the minor chord shape with the barre across the 2nd fret

Instant B minor chord!

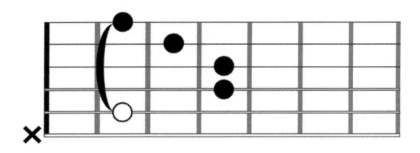

For a **C# minor** chord:

- Find **C#** on the A string (find it at the **4th** fret)
- Play the minor chord shape with the barre across the 4th fret

Instant C# minor chord!

Changing the Major Shape into a Dominant 7 Chord

We can also re-finger the major shape and use it to play dominant 7 chords. Here's the 7 chord shape below:

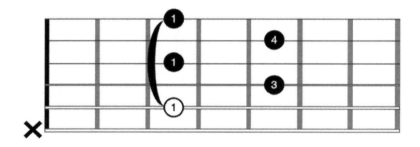

So, if you needed to play an **E7** chord:

- Find **E** on the A string. It's at the **7th** fret
- Play the 7 chord shape with the barre across the 7th fret

Instant E7 chord!

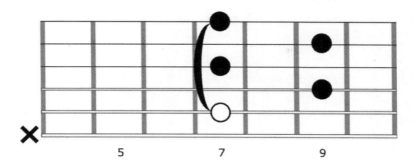

For a **Bb7** chord:

- Find **Bb** on the A string. It's at the **1st** fret
- Play the 7 chord shape with the barre across the 1st fret

Instant Bb7 chord!

Here's a recap of what you've learned so far in this chapter:

- You know the **A shape barre chord** shape for playing a **major** chord
- You know how the **chord shape, root note** and the **notes** on the A string work together to give you **any major chord**
- You know the **A shape barre chord** to use for playing a **minor** chord
- You know the **A shape barre chord** to use for playing a **7** chord
- You can see how all this can be used to play *any* major, minor or 7 chord there is!

Use The Following Practical Exercises to Master This Chapter

Here are **4 simple exercises** to help you to consolidate, understand and apply what you've learned in this chapter.

By spending **3 to 5 minutes** on **4 exercises** each day, your practice will quickly pay off and you'll soon be fluent with this set of barre chords. If they don't sound perfect yet, don't get frustrated! Get them sounding as good as you can, practice regularly and you'll soon notice a difference.

Exercise 1: Throw Away the Major Shape

- Make the major A shape barre chord at any fret you like
- Use the **'Throwing Away'** exercise to thoroughly learn it
- Repeat over and over, periodically moving to a different fret

Exercise 2: Throw Away the Minor and Dominant 7 Shapes

- Repeat the above exercise for the minor chord shape
- Repeat the above exercise for the dominant 7 chord shape

Exercise 3: Note Finding

- Using the following fretboard diagram, memorise the notes B, C, D and E along the A string. If you have dots/fret markers along the neck of your guitar, use them to help
- Now learn where to find F, G and A
- Once you know these notes, learn the sharp (#) and flat (b) notes too

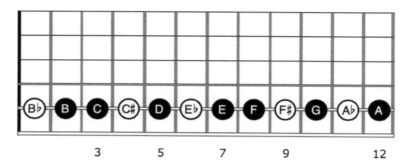

Exercise 4: Chord Finding

- Using the A shape major, minor and 7 barre shapes, play the following sequences of chords:
    - B major to Bm to B7
    - C major to Cm to C7
    - D major to Dm to D7
    - E major to Em to E7
    - F major to Fm to F7
    - G major to Gm to G7

Quick Quiz

Test yourself with this quiz. Check your answers on the following page.

Play the following major, minor or 7 chords using the A shape barre chords from this chapter:

C
E7
Bm
D
Fm
G
E*b*7
C#m
B*b*
F#m

Find Out How You Did!

C (3rd fret major shape)
E7 (7th fret 7 shape)
Bm (2nd fret minor shape)
D (5th fret major shape)
Fm (8th fret minor shape)
G (10th fret major shape)
Eb7 (6th fret 7 shape)
C#m (4th fret minor shape)
Bb (1st fret major shape)
F#m (9th fret minor shape)

Have You Reached Your Goals?

Let's see how you did with the goals we set at the start of this chapter. Check off each one when you're confident you've achieved it.

If you need to go back and spend some more time on a topic then do.

I can play the 'A shape' major barre chord [   ]

I can play the 'A shape' minor barre chord [   ]

I can play the 'A shape' 7 barre chord [   ]

I can use the A string root note to play 36 possible chords [   ]

Checked all the goals off?

Congratulations!

When you're ready move on to the next chapter where we're going to look at using these A shape barre chords in the music you play. We'll look at switching between different A shape barre chords, combining them with open chords and more.

Look forward to seeing you then!

Chapter 4: A Shape Barre Chord Training

Welcome to Chapter 4.

Now that you understand A shape barre chords it's time to practice moving them around and connecting them up to play chord sequences. You also need to practice combining them with the basic open chords.

Then, just as with the E shape chords, you'll be able to use A shape barre chords fluently when you play guitar.

As before we'll be using a **3 Step Plan** to accomplish all this and it will help you achieve the following goals:

1. You'll be fluent at moving A shape barre chords around the neck

2. You'll be able to switch between major, minor and 7 chords using the A shape barre chord

3. You'll be able to change between A shape barre chords and various open chord shapes

Don't forget the **3 Golden Rules** when it comes to changing between chords. They are:

Rule 1: Know The Chord Shapes... *Thoroughly!*
Rule 2: See Where You're Going... *Before* **it's Time to Move!**
Rule 3: Only Move the Fingers That *Need* **To Move!**

Grab your guitar and let's get started!

The 3 Step Plan for Mastering A Shape Barre Chords

With this 3 Step Plan you can soon become an expert at using the A shape barre chords in your playing. Go through the steps in order using the exercises and guidelines given.

Spend 10-15 minutes on the 3 Step Plan each day to see good results quickly.

Let's move onto the first step.

Step 1: Moving the Same Barre Chord

As before we'll practice moving the major shape first. Then we'll do the same with the minor and dominant 7 shapes.

Moving the Major Chord Shape

We've seen how there are a few different options when it comes to fingering this chord shape. Whichever one you choose to use, the method of learning to move it around is the same.

Let's use the major A shape barre chord to play a C chord at the 3rd fret:

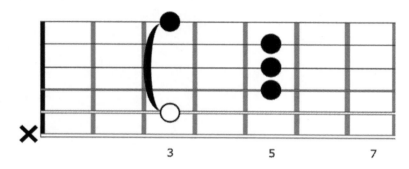

Now we'll use the same shape to play D at the 5th fret:

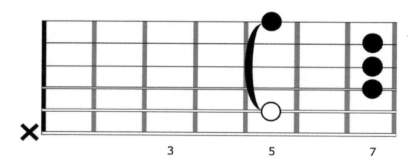

Then practice slowly switching between them. A quick reminder about the best way to do this:

1. Play the C chord at the 3rd fret
2. Now look ahead and 'see' the D chord at the 5th fret
3. Relax the C chord so you're not pressing down but *leave your fingers in the shape of the chord*
4. Now the chord shape is relaxed, gently shift it up to the 5th fret trying to maintain the chord shape with your fingers
5. Now press it down again to get the D chord
6. Now follow the exact same process to change back down to C again

Repeat this exercise 5-6 times and remember to do each chord changing exercise *without* any rhythmic strumming to begin with. Add strumming only when you can change the chord without any problems.

Remember, when adding strumming, start as slowly and simply as you need to. Also, remember not to let your strumming hand 'wait' for the chord hand!

Apply the chord changing exercise (both with and without strumming) to the following pairs of major chords:

Bb (1st fret) to **C** (3rd fret)
D (5th fret) to **E** (7th fret)
B (2nd fret) to **C#** (4th fret)

Moving the Minor Chord Shape

Now let's practice using the minor chord shape below to change between various minor chords:

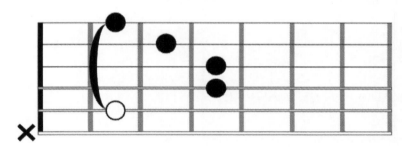

Using the minor barre chord shape, practice changing between the following pairs of minor chords. You'll probably find this shape easier to move around than the major shape!

Follow the method and guidelines you used before:

Bbm (1st fret) to **Cm** (3rd fret)
Cm (3rd fret) to **Dm** (5th fret)
Dm (5th fret) to **Em** (7th fret)
Bm (2nd fret) to **C#m** (4th fret)

Moving the 7 Chord Shape

Finally, let's practice using the 7 chord shape to change between different dominant 7 chords. Here's a reminder of the 7 chord shape you need:

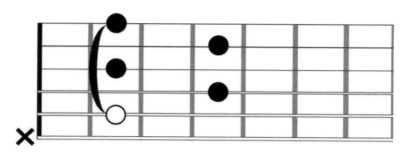

Practice changing between these pairs of 7 chords. Use the method and guidelines we used for the major and minor shapes:

D7 (5th fret) to **E7** (7th fret)
C7 (3rd fret) to **D7** (5th fret)
B7 (2nd fret) to **C#7** (4th fret)
E7 (7th fret) to **G7** (10th fret)

Step 2: Moving Between Different Shapes

Once you're comfortable moving the same barre chord shape around, you can start mixing up the major, minor and dominant 7 shapes.

Changing Between Major and Minor

Let's use the major barre chord shape to play a C chord at the 3rd fret:

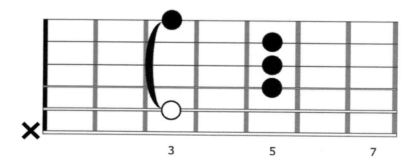

Now use the minor barre shape to play Dm at the 5th fret:

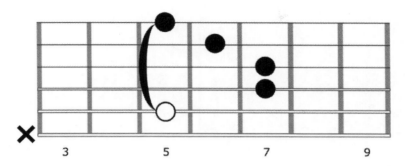

Practice switching between these 5-6 times. Look ahead, maintain the chord shape with your fingers, and follow all the other guidelines we talked about earlier.

Changing Between Major and 7

Let's use the major barre chord shape to play a B*b* chord at the 1st fret:

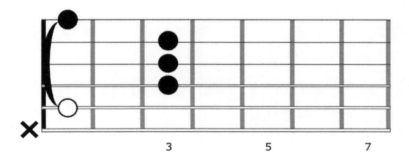

Now use the 7 barre shape to play C7 at the 3rd fret:

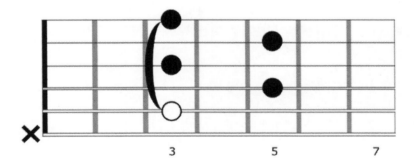

Slowly and accurately practice switching between these chords 5-6 times.

Changing Between Minor and 7

Let's use the minor barre chord shape to play an Em chord at the 7th fret:

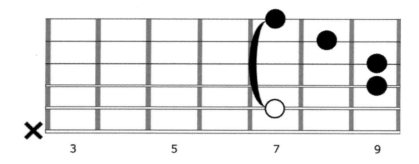

Now use the 7 barre shape to play D7 at the 5th fret:

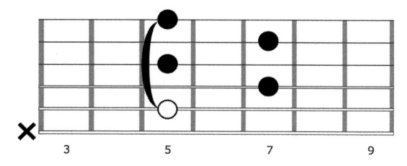

Practice switching between them 5-6 times, adding some strumming when you feel ready.

Combining All 3 Shapes!

Remember, you can practice the following exercises along to the free audio tracks which come with this book – visit this page to get them: **jamesshipwayguitar.com/barre-chords-audio**

Now, let's have a go at mixing up all the A shape barre chord shapes we've covered so far. From now on I won't be telling you which fret to move the shapes to, I'll be leaving this part to you.

To start, try changing from Em to D to C to D7 with one bar on each chord:

Start by slowly practicing switching from shape to shape, before adding any rhythm or strumming. When the exercise feels easy, loop it round and round as if you were playing a song using these chords.

Here are some more exercises to get you mixing up different chords. Play each chord only with the major, minor or 7 variation of the A shape barre chord:

| C / / / | Dm / / / | Em / / / | F / / / | ▶ **Audio Track 4.2**

| C / / / | F / / / | Em / / / | Dm / / / | ▶ **Audio Track 4.3**

| B / / / | D#7 / / / | E / / / | C#m / / / | ▶ **Audio Track 4.4**

| Dm / / / | F / / / | B♭ / / / | C / / / | ▶ **Audio Track 4.5**

| B♭m / / / | D♭ / / / | F#7 / / / | F7 / / / | ▶ **Audio Track 4.6**

Take your time and follow all the guidelines given as you work on each of the examples above.

When you can play through these comfortably then you're well on your way to mastering the A shape barre chords!

If you're ready move on to Step 3.

Step 3: Combining Barre Chords and Open Chords

In a lot of situations, you'll want to combine the big, resonant sound of open chords, with the portability and flexibility of barre chords. Learning to do this is the focus of this final step.

Changing from an open chord to a barre chord (or vice-versa) normally requires a little more work from our chord hand than moving the same barre chord shape around the neck does, but once you're fluent at using barre chord shapes, most chord changes are pretty easy.

Work through the exercises that follow to become fluent at combining open chords and barre chords. Remember to start slow, look ahead to see where you're moving your fingers to and watch for any fingers which are in the same place for both shapes and can be left in place. Add strumming *only* when the chord changes are smooth!

(**Note:** If you're unsure of the shapes for any of the open chord shapes here then see the appendix at the end of this book).

Two Chord Changes

Let's start by changing between only two chords. Practice the basic chord changing move first. Then when you're ready, play 2 bars on each chord and loop the resulting 4 bar chord sequence round and round.

When it feels easy, start playing 1 bar on each chord, then change to the next one.

Use the following exercises:

G (open chord shape) to **C** (barre shape)

|: G / / / | G / / / | C / / / | C / / / :|

▶ **Audio Track 4.7**

Am (open chord shape) to **C** (barre shape)

|: Am / / / | Am / / / | C / / / | C / / / :|

▶ **Audio Track 4.8**

E (open chord shape) to **B** (barre shape)

|: E / / / | E / / / | B / / / | B / / / :|

▶ **Audio Track 4.9**

G (open chord shape) to **Bm** (barre shape)

|: G / / / | G / / / | Bm / / / | Bm / / / :|

▶ **Audio Track 4.10**

Dm (open chord shape) to **Bb7** (barre shape)

|: Dm / / / | Dm / / / | Bb7 / / / | Bb7 / / / :|

▶ **Audio Track 4.11**

C (open chord shape) to **Bb** (barre shape)

|: C / / / | C / / / | Bb / / / | Bb / / / :|

▶ **Audio Track 4.12**

Dm (barre shape) to **A** (open chord shape)

|: Dm / / / | Dm / / / | A / / / | A / / / :|

▶ **Audio Track 4.13**

Bm (barre shape) to **D** (open chord shape)

|: Bm / / / | Bm / / / | D / / / | D / / / :| ▶ **Audio Track 4.14**

When you've got the hang of these move on.

More Complex Chord Sequences

Now apply all the same practice techniques and methods to the common chord sequences below. Some of them can be played just using open chords, but this won't help you master barre chords! So, be sure to use the open chord and A barre chord shapes as indicated.

G (open) **Bm** (barre) **C** (open) **D** (open)

|: G / / / | Bm / / / | C / / / | D / / / :| ▶ **Audio Track 4.15**

A (open) **Bm** (barre) **C#m** (barre) **D** (open)

|: A / / / | Bm / / / | C#m / / / | D / / / :| ▶ **Audio Track 4.16**

D (open) **G** (open) **Bm** (barre) **A** (open)

|: D / / / | G / / / | Bm / / / | A / / / :| ▶ **Audio Track 4.17**

E (open) **C#m** (barre) **B** (barre) **A** (open)

|: E / / / | C#m / / / | B / / / | A / / / :| ▶ **Audio Track 4.18**

Dm (barre) **C** (barre) **B♭7** (barre) **A** (open)

|: Dm / / / | C / / / | B♭7 / / / | A / / / :| ▶ **Audio Track 4.19**

Have You Reached Your Goals?

If you can play smoothly through all the examples in this chapter then you can use both the E shape *and* A shape barre chords fluently. This is a huge achievement; in fact you've now done most of the hard work and you're well on your way to mastering barre chords!

Let's see how you did with the goals we set at the start of this chapter. Check off each one when you're confident you've achieved it.

I am fluent at moving A shape barre chords around the neck   [ ]

I can switch between major, minor and 7 chords using the A shape barre chord   [ ]

I can change between A shape barre chords and various open chord shapes (and use them together to play chord sequences) [ ]

I can apply strumming patterns whilst changing between multiple chords (both open shapes and barre shapes) [ ]

Checked all the goals off?

Awesome!

In the next chapter we're going to look at combining E and A shape barre chords so that you can freely mix them up whenever you need to. When you can do this, you'll have the barre chord skills that most guitarists use 95% of the time.

You're into the final stages of your journey towards barre chord mastery now.

When you're ready, let's move on to Chapter 5!

Chapter 5: Combining E and A Shape Barre Chords

With the E and A shapes you have most of the barre chord knowledge you need. This chapter will help you learn to use these two shapes in any combination. Being able to do this will give you the ability to play a huge range of different songs as well as write music of your own, without hunting around wondering how to play the chords you need!

By the end of this chapter you'll have achieved the following goals:

1. You'll be fluent at changing from any E shape barre chord into any A shape barre chord and vice-versa

2. You'll be able to choose the best combinations of barre chords to get the sound you want to hear

3. You'll be able to fluently mix up open chord, E shape and A shape barre chords to play thousands of songs and chord sequences!

Grab your guitar and let's get started!

The Power of Combining E and A Barre Chord Shapes...

By knowing E and A shape barre chords you have *two* places on the neck to play any major, minor or 7 chord.

For example, a B major chord could be played at the 7th fret using the E shape barre chord:

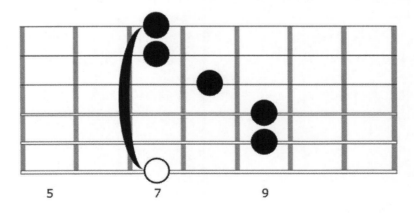

Or it could be played at the 2nd fret using the A shape barre chord:

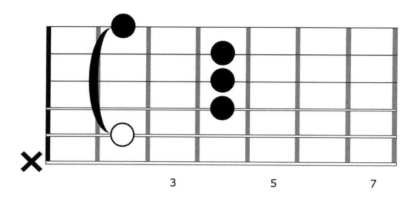

Of course, by changing the shapes slightly, B minor or B7 chords could also be played at these frets.

What this means is that you have a choice about *where* you play a chord on the neck.

This is very useful. It means you can play a chord at the easiest and most convenient location on the neck depending on the situation.

For example, imagine you were playing the following chord progression:

| G / / / | D / / / | Bm / / / | C / / / |

Let's say you were using open chords to play G, D and C. Jumping all the way up to the 7th fret to play Bm would be a bit illogical and possibly break the flow of the music. It makes much more sense to play Bm at the 2nd fret because it's closer on the guitar to the other chords.

Playing chord shapes which are close together in this way normally makes for an easier change and a smoother sound from chord to chord. As we'll see in this chapter, combining E and A shape barre chords makes it easy to achieve this most of the time.

You might also choose where to play a chord based on the sound. Playing a Bm chord at the 7th fret with an E shape barre chord sounds slightly different to playing it at the 2nd fret with the A shape barre chord. Chords played around the lower frets tend to give you a bigger, warmer sound and often work well in a chord sequence. Once you get above the 5th fret, barre chords tend to sound brighter and 'thinner', but they're still useful because sometimes this might be just the sound you're after!

Combining E and A shape barre chords is not hard to do once you're comfortable with the basic barre shapes (which you are by now!). So, grab your guitar and let's start mixing things up...

First, a quick word of warning…

If you're unsure about root notes and which fret to play an E or A shape barre chord to get a certain chord, then you're not quite ready for what we're about to cover. If this is you, don't worry, just go back to the earlier chapters and recap on this information… it will help you sail through this chapter problem-free!

Changing Between E and A Shape Barre Chords

Let's start by practicing some simple two chord combinations to get you used to switching between E and A shape barre chords.

As you go through these remember to:

- Look ahead for the chord you're changing to (see it on the guitar neck)
- Leave fingers down when possible (including the finger playing the barre)
- Relax the shape and keep as much of it intact when moving to a different fret. Do this even when changing to a different type of barre chord (i.e. E shape to A shape or vice-versa)
- Add in strumming of your choice when you can change between the shapes without any problems

With all this in mind, practice changing backwards and forwards between the following combinations of barre chords. They've been arranged into sets, each one developing a different skill. Go through each set one at a time mastering the chord changes in each. Fret locations aren't given (you know these by now!).

Set 1

A (E shape barre) to **D** (A shape barre)

A (E shape barre) to **C#m** (A shape barre)

A (E shape barre) to **E7** (A shape barre)

Set 2

C (A shape barre) to **Am** (E shape barre)

Dm (A shape barre) to **Am** (E shape barre)

E7 (A shape barre) to **Am** (E shape barre)

Set 3

G7 (E shape barre) to **C7** (A shape barre)

A7 (E shape barre) to **D** (A shape barre)

F7 (E shape barre) to **B***b***m** (A shape barre)

Combining Shapes to Play Common Chord Sequences

Once you can play through the three sets of chord changes I just gave you, then playing through chord progressions or songs with barre chords is almost no different. Practice the chord progressions coming up next. Choose your own speed and strumming to make each one sound the way you want it to!

For playing this example use an E shape barre chord for **A** and **G** and an A shape for **C#m** and **Bm**.

|: A / / / | C#m / / / | G / / / | Bm / / / :| ▶ **Audio Track 5.1**

For the next example use the E shape barre chord for **G** and **B***b***7** and an A shape for **Dm** and **C**.

|: Dm / / / | G / / / | B*b*7 / / / | C / / / :| ▶ **Audio Track 5.2**

Play this longer example using an E shape barre chord for **G, Bm** and **Am**. Play **C, D** and **Em** with an A shape barre chord.

|: G / / / | D / / / | Em / / / | C / / / |

| Bm / / / | D / / / | Am / / / |C / / / :| ▶ **Audio Track 5.3**

Now *you* choose whether to use an E shape or an A shape barre chord! Work out some of the different ways of playing each chord sequence. Try to use shapes which are close together on the neck to avoid awkward changes and make sure to use a mixture of A and E shapes so that you're practicing using both.

|: F / / / | Gm / / / | B*b* / / / | Gm / / / :| ▶ **Audio Track 5.4**

|: Cm / / / | A*b* / / / | E*b* / / / | B*b* / / / :| ▶ **Audio Track 5.5**

|: D / A / | Bm / G / | D / A / | G / A / :| ▶ **Audio Track 5.6**

When you've done all these with barre chords, you could also try working some open chords in as well. This will help you integrate all your open chords and barre chords together into one big chord vocabulary which you can use easily and fluently!

Have You Reached Your Goals?

If you can comfortably play all the examples in this chapter smoothly then it's safe to say that you've pretty much nailed the most essential barre chords you need to know. Awesome work!

Your next step is to seek out songs which you've always wanted to play and learn them. The chances are, many of them will use a mixture of open chords and barre chords and playing them will help you further strengthen your barre chord skills.

If you're a songwriter or composer (or if you want to become one!), try composing some chord sequences similar to the examples I've given you here. Mix them up, repeat bits, make them longer, change chords around or do anything else you want. Remember, if it sounds good to you, then it's right!

Let's see how you did with the goals we set at the start of this chapter. Check off each one when you're sure you've achieved it.

I feel like I'm fluent at changing from any E shape barre chord to any A shape barre chord and vice-versa [ ]

I can see the different options about where to play a particular chord and am able choose the best combinations of barre chords to get the sound I want to hear [   ]

I feel confident that I can now fluently mix up open chords, E shape and A shape barre chords and use this skill to play thousands of potential songs and chord sequences!...[   ]

Checked all the goals off?

Excellent!

Before we wrap up, there are some other useful barre chord shapes I think you ought to know, and we're going to cover those in the next chapter. Most of them are simply variations on the E and A shape chords we've already seen, so playing them will be plain sailing!

When you're ready move on to Chapter 6.

Chapter 6: The D Shape Barre Chord and Other Useful Shapes

This chapter is going to build on all the barre chord knowledge you've gained so far and show you some other useful barre chords. Many guitar players get by with just the E and A shapes and depending on the kind of music you play you may not ever need to know what's in this chapter, but because you've made it this far into this book I'm guessing you can see the awesome power of barre chords and you want to learn more about them!

By the end of this chapter, you'll have achieved the following goals:

1. You'll know how to play and use D shape barre chords

2. You'll be able to convert the E, A and D barre chord shapes into other useful chords which you may see from time to time

3. You'll have some knowledge of how and when to use some of these barre chord variations

So, let's get started!

The D Shape Barre Chords

One barre chord shape we haven't looked at yet is the D shape barre chord. Most guitarists don't use this as often as the E and A shape chords, but it's still useful to know.

The D shape barre chords have their root note on the D string and only use the top four strings of the guitar. Because the E and A strings aren't played they have a bright, trebly sound which can be useful in certain situations. Other times they may lack the depth and bass you need, it all depends on the sound you're looking for.

Let's take a look at the shapes.

Use this shape to play a major chord:

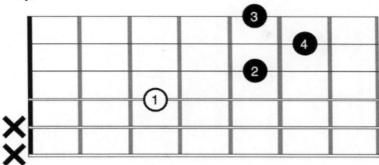

Use this shape to play a minor chord:

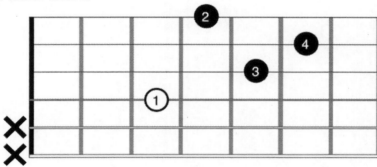

Use this shape to play a 7 chord:

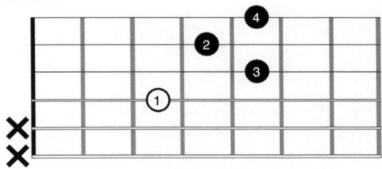

Practice the '**Throwing Away**' Exercise to get these shapes under your fingers. You probably noticed how the major shape uses an awkward fret hand stretch! If this is difficult at first, move the shape higher up the neck where the frets are closer together to make the stretch smaller. Persevere. Practice the shape regularly and you'll soon find it begins to get easier.

'Pairing Up' D and E Shape Chords

I'm going to show you an easy way to learn where to play the D shape barre chords to help you become fluent at using them.

Here's an easy rule to remember:

Any note on the low E string can also be found 2 frets higher up on the D string.

For example, G is at the 3rd fret on the low E string, so we can also find a G at the 5th fret (2 frets up) on the D string.

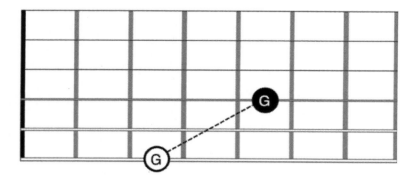

By knowing the E shape barre chords you can easily find how to play the same chord using the D shape; just play it 2 frets higher.

Here is G played with an E shape chord:

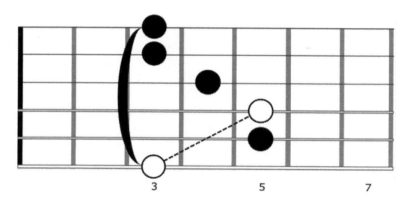

... and below is G played with a D shape chord (the G note on the E string is marked with a black diamond to help you see the connection between the shapes):

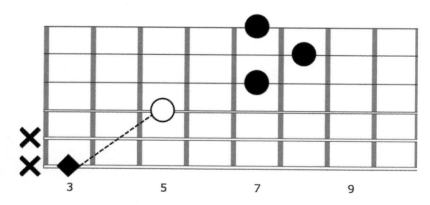

'Pairing' these shapes up in this way makes it easier to find the D shape chords. It also builds a connection between them and makes it easier to start using a D shape instead of an E shape sometimes.

Use This Practical Exercise to Master D Shape Chords

Once you've got to grips with the D shape chords, take some of the chord sequence exercises in the previous chapters and practice inserting some D shape barre chords where you were previously playing an E shape.

Some of the changes may be a little tricky at first. If so, just remember that E and A shape chords were also tricky to start with! Isolate and practice any difficult chord changes until they don't hold you up anymore.

After a little while, you'll have another powerful tool in your barre chord armoury!

Other Useful Barre Chords

To play many styles of music you don't need anything more than simple major, minor and 7 chords, but sometimes you may need to play a slightly more complex chord, for example a minor7 or 7sus4 chord.

Whilst this may sound scary, the good news is that with a simple tweak, the barre chords you've learned so far can be adapted to play other chords as well. In some cases it's as simple as lifting off one finger (easy huh?).

The remainder of this chapter will teach you some other barre chord shapes which you'll find useful to know. This is not supposed to be an in depth study of complex jazz chords or chord harmony! It's just a basic supplement to what you've already learned in this book.

Normally these more complex chords simply act as a 'stand in' or a 'substitute' for a basic major, minor or 7 chord. For example, instead of playing a basic A minor chord, a songwriter might choose to use an A minor7 chord instead (more on these in a moment).

Why?

Just because it creates a different mood and sound in the music and he or she prefers the sound of it. It's a way of 'decorating' the sound of a chord. It's as simple as that... we don't need to over complicate it!

You can try using some of these chords in any songs you play. Listen carefully to hear if they work or not. Guidelines are helpful, but we need to use our ears to make the final decision about whether something sounds right or wrong.

For most of these chords I've given you one shape for the E, A and D string root notes. In some cases a practical shape isn't available and I've left one of these out.

To make these shapes easier to learn and remember, think of them as *variations* on the basic E, A and D shape barre chords. They may look and sound a bit different, but making this connection between them will help them to stick in your memory and make them much easier to find when you need them.

Let's look at some new chord types and some guidelines for how to use them. Suggested fingerings are given for each shape but feel free to vary these as you wish. Root notes are shown as a white disc on the diagrams.

'Suspended 4th' Chords

These are written as **sus4** and normally stand in for basic major chords. For example, a **Csus4** chord could stand in for a basic **C** chord. It's also very common to mix both types of chords together. For example, 2 bars on a C chord could become:

| C / Csus4 / | C / Csus4 / |

Here are some handy sus4 chord shapes:

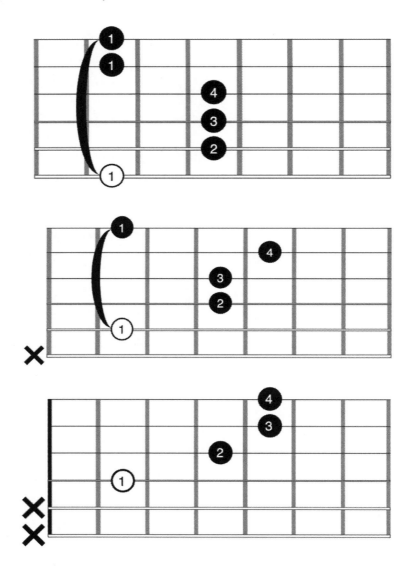

'Suspended 2nd' Chords

These are written as **sus2** and normally stand in for basic major chords. For example, a **Dsus2** chord could stand in for a basic **D** chord. Just like sus4 chords, you can mix both types of chords together. For example, 2 bars on a C chord could become:

| C / Csus2 / | C / Csus2 / |

Here are some handy sus2 chord shapes:

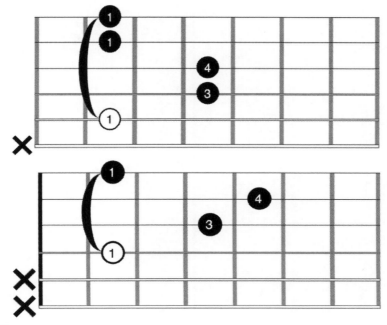

'Major Seventh' Chords

These are normally written as **Major7** or **Maj7** and can stand in for basic major chords. For example, a **Cmaj7** chord could stand in for a **C** chord. Sometimes this won't sound good though, so let your ears be the final judge.

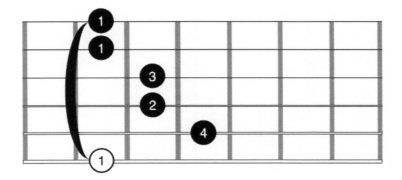

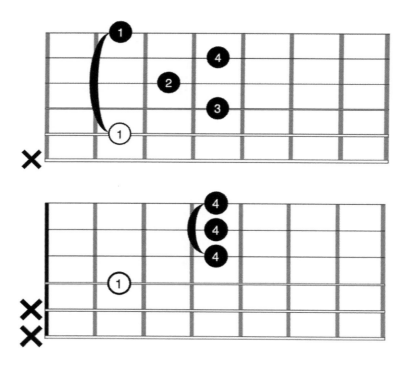

'Minor Seventh' Chords

These are normally written as **m7** and can stand in for basic minor chords. For example, an **Em7** chord can often stand in for a basic **Em** chord.

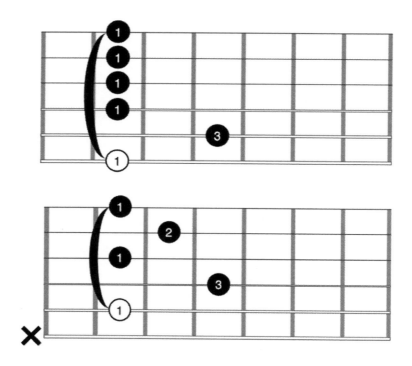

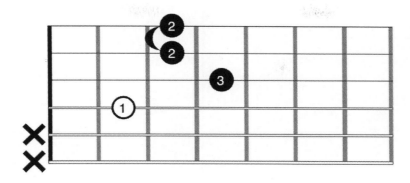

'Dominant 7 Suspended 4th' Chords

These are normally written as **7sus4** and stand in for **7** chords. For example, an **F7sus4** chord might stand in for a plain **F7** chord. It's also common to mix both sounds up.

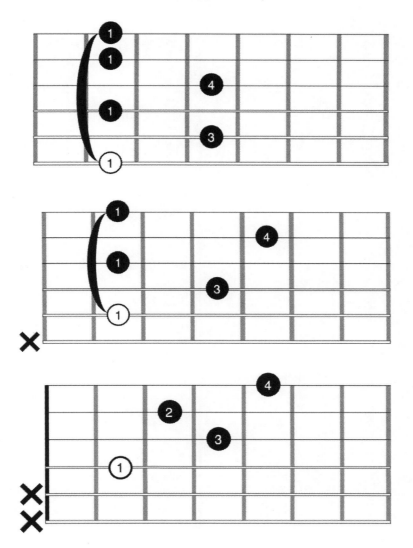

'Major add9' Chords

These are normally written as **add9** and stand in for basic major chords. For example, a **Gadd9** chord could stand in for a basic **G** chord. This is a very effective way to add a more 'lush' sound to a simple major chord and is a trick that is used a lot. The stretches in these shapes are difficult. Relax your hand and persevere!

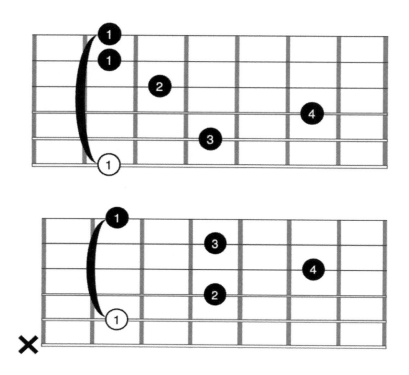

'Minor add9' Chords

These are normally written as **madd9** and stand in for basic minor chords. For example, an **Amadd9** chord could stand in for a plain **Am** chord. Doing this adds an intense, moody sound to a simple minor chord, try it and see! The stretches in these shapes will take some practice. Relax your hand and persevere!

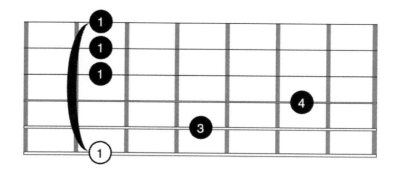

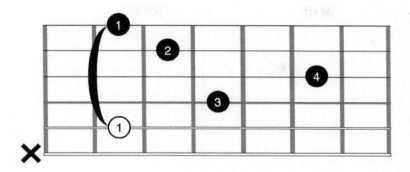

Have You Reached Your Goals?

Let's see how you did with the goals we set at the start of this chapter. Check off each one when you're sure you've achieved it.

I know how to play D shape barre chords and can 'pair' them up to E shape chords   [   ]

I know barre chord shapes for some other useful chords   [   ]

I have some knowledge of how and when to use some of these barre chord variations   [   ]

Checked all the goals off?

Awesome! You now have an excellent knowledge of the most common variations on the basic barre chord shapes. So, the next time you see a chord symbol like Am7, Cmaj7 or F#7sus 4 you'll know exactly how to approach playing it.

You've also been given helpful guidelines about how these more colourful chords are often used.

So now it's your turn. Take some of these chords and experiment with using them in music you already play. Swap basic major, minor and 7 chords for their more colourful 'stand in' chords and notice how it changes the sound. You might find that these alternative chords really help to bring your music to life and make it stand out from the crowd.

Have fun experimenting and remember if it sounds right, it is right!

Final Words

Congratulations!

You've reached the end of *No Bull Barre Chords for Guitar*!

I hope you feel that you now have the knowledge and understanding you need to use barre chords confidently in any of the music you play.

If you need to revisit any part of this book then do so. Go over each chapter as many times as necessary for it to make total sense. The better you understand everything I've showed you, the better you'll be at applying it fluently when you play your guitar.

It's important to actually *use* what you have learned here. This is the only way you'll get everything off these pages and into your playing!

Find and learn songs which use barre chords, try using barre chord shapes instead of open chords, make up your own barre chord exercises... and do anything else you can think of which will help you get 100% confident with these powerful chord shapes.

I hope you've enjoyed learning with me. If you have, let me know (info@headstockbooks.com). If you could spare five minutes to leave a review on whichever platform you bought this book from, I'd be most grateful. It helps the book and it helps me too!

Remember to check out the **Useful Resources** section to find out more about my other books, video courses and my *Total Guitar Lab* online membership/coaching site.

So, keep practising, have fun and I'll see you next time!

James

Free Audio Tracks

Don't forget to grab the audio practice tracks which accompany this book. They'll help you master barre chords in your playing. The audio tracks are recordings of selected exercises from *No Bull Barre Chords for Guitar*. Download them, and you can play along with me, just like in an actual guitar lesson. They'll be great for helping your timing, strumming and chord changing skills!

Grab your audio tracks for free here: **jamesshipwayguitar.com/barre-chords-audio**

Useful Open Chord Shapes

Here you'll find some common open chord shapes. You can use these to play the exercises in *No Bull Barre Chords for Guitar* which combine barre chords and open chords.

<u>**Common Open Chords**</u>

G

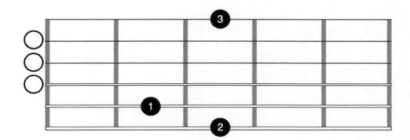

D

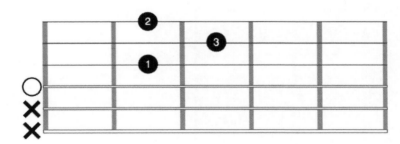

C

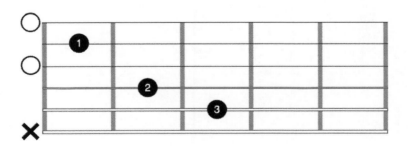

A

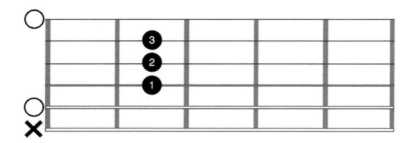

E

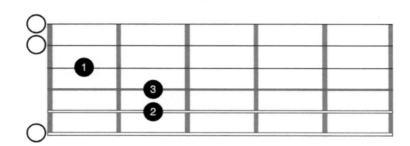

F

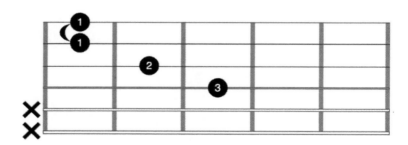

Em

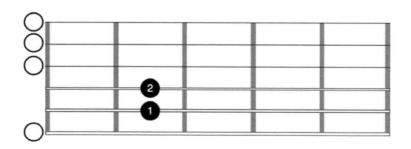

Am

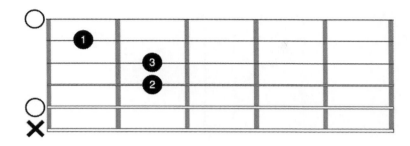

Dm

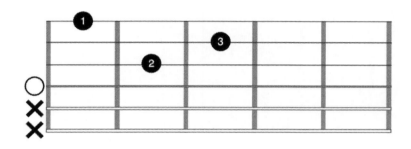

E7

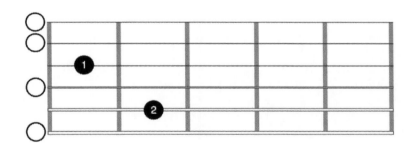

A7

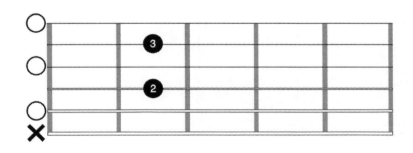

D7

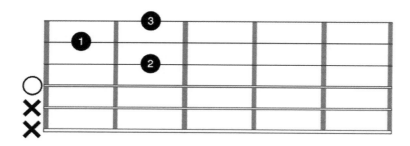

B7

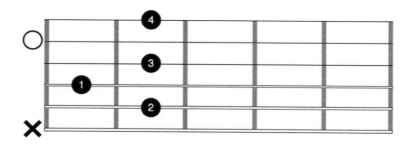

G7

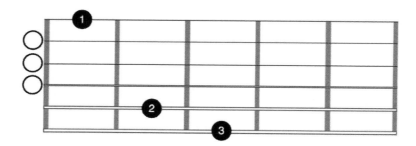

Useful Resources

Other Books by James Shipway:

Below you will find a list of my other guitar books. To find out more about each one, or to see where you can order from, please visit Headstock Books at:

headstockbooks.com

Most titles are available as paperbacks, ebooks and hardcovers from Amazon, Apple, Google Play, Kobo, Barnes & Noble, and by request from your local library or book shop.

'No Bull Music Theory for Guitarists'

Master the essential music theory knowledge all guitarists need to know with the original **'No Bull Music Theory for Guitarists'**, the first of three books in the **Music Theory for Guitarists** series. Understand chords, keys, intervals, scales and more and become a better **musician, guitarist and songwriter**. In a few short hours this book gives you the knowledge that most guitar players take years to accumulate ...and many never truly understand. **Free audiobook version included**!

'Music Theory for Guitarists, Volume 2'

Continue your journey towards music theory and guitar fretboard mastery with the second book in the **Music Theory for Guitarists** series. Discover 'sus' and 'add9' chords, compound intervals, seventh chords, key signatures, the modes of the major scale, triad chord inversions, using the circle of fifths and much more. Packed full of practical exercises and examples and **includes downloadable play-along tracks**.

'Music Theory for Guitarists, Volume 3'

Take your music theory expertise and understanding of the guitar fretboard *even* further with the third book in the **Music Theory for Guitarists** series! Learn about the CAGED System, soloing with modes, chord substitution tricks and techniques, minor key progressions and improvisation, the harmonic minor scale, extended chords, key change and modulation techniques and much more. Packed full of practical exercises and examples and **includes downloadable play-along tracks**.

'Blues Soloing for Guitar', Volumes 1 & 2

Volume 1: 'Blues Basics' A step-by-step introduction for learning to play blues guitar, featuring the essential techniques, scales and theory you need to know, as well as complete solos in the styles of important blues legends.

Volume 2: 'Levelling Up' This book carries on where Volume 1 leaves off. It features lessons on minor blues soloing, open string soloing and scales, Texas blues style and 'jazzy' blues sounds and more.

Both books include access to a supporting website with **video lessons and audio downloads**.

'The CAGED System for Guitar'

A step-by-step method showing you how to master the guitar fretboard using the CAGED System to become a better lead player, improviser and all round guitarist.

Discover how the CAGED System works and how to use it to learn all the scales and arpeggios you need to know to become an awesome guitar player. With crystal clear explanations, practice exercises and tips, 'speed learning' techniques, as well as dozens of exciting sample licks, **'The CAGED System for Guitar'** can seriously transform your playing skills. Includes **downloadable video demonstrations and backing tracks.**

'Circle of Fifths for Guitar'

Discover the awesome power of the circle of fifths and use it to **boost your guitar skills, music theory knowledge, song writing skills** ...and more! Bite-sized lessons showing you how to use the circle of fifths to memorise the notes on the guitar fretboard, practice smarter for faster progress, learn the chords in every major and minor key, change keys quickly and easily, understand chord progressions and songs, and much more. With practical exercises and quizzes to check your understanding. Includes a downloadable **circle of fifths video masterclass**!

'The Guitar Practice Workbook'

The ultimate **'multi-purpose' practice workbook** for guitarists of all levels. Featuring powerful practice hacks, important scales and chord shapes as well as over 50 pages of blank tab, fretboard diagrams and chord boxes for recording your own killer licks, exercises and song ideas! Available with **free downloadable 'Goal Worksheet'** to help you track your progress and reach your guitar goals! Available as a paperback only.

Check Out My *Total Guitar Lab* Online School

Want to study specific guitar styles and topics with me as your guitar teacher? Well you can, with my online guitar community **Total Guitar Lab**! Join and get instant access to *all* my premium guitar courses *plus* live training, workshops and Q&A sessions. Learn more and discover the amazing results guitarists have been getting with my training. Visit **totalguitarlab.com**

Single Courses Also Available:

Some of my guitar courses are available as stand-alone products. This means they are yours to keep and go through at your own pace as many times as you like.

Courses are made up of step-by-step video lessons, downloadable backing tracks, audio lessons and detailed tab workbooks complete with homework tasks and checklists to make sure you reach your goals.

The following courses are currently available. You can find them at **totalguitarlab.com** :

Blues Guitar Launchpad

The perfect course for the beginner to intermediate electric blues guitarist. Learn all the essential blues scales, how to play the 12 bar blues, authentic blues licks, string bending and vibrato techniques plus complete solo studies in the styles of blues legends like Eric Clapton, Stevie Ray Vaughan, Freddie King, Otis Rush and others! Learn more at: **totalguitarlab.com**

Minor Pentatonic Mastery

Perfect for the more experienced rock or blues player who wants to conquer the minor pentatonic scale all over the guitar neck! *Minor Pentatonic Mastery* takes you step-by-step through all the ways to play the minor pentatonic scale on the guitar. Learn all 5 'box patterns' and how to use them to play killer blues and rock licks, discover 'sliding' scale patterns, the 'Rule of 2' to use for connecting it all up and loads more powerful soloing and improvising tips to use in building an awesome pentatonic soloing vocabulary. Learn more at: **totalguitarlab.com**

Rock Guitar Lick Lab

Aimed at the intermediate rock guitar player who wants to explode their playing with the licks and techniques used by the biggest names in rock and metal guitar. Discover essential rock bending licks, repeating licks, alternate picked licks, extended blues scale licks and stretch and sequence licks and how to use them in your playing for explosive rock and metal guitar solos!

You'll also learn essential technique tips to get the licks sounding great and how to use everything in the course to easily start generating killer rock licks of your own. Learn more at: **totalguitarlab.com**

Solo Blues Jamming Workshop

Learn a step-by-step method for combining chords and licks into your very own solo blues jams! Includes play-a-long tracks, drill videos and more to help you master this fun way of playing blues guitar. Learn more at: **totalguitarlab.com**

Notebuster

Want to learn all the notes on the fretboard in the quickest and most pain free way possible? *Notebuster* will show you how! After this short mini course, you'll be able to find *any* note on *any* string … *anywhere* on the guitar. Learn more at: **totalguitarlab.com**

Follow me on YouTube:

Search for James Shipway Guitar on YouTube and subscribe for hours of free video lessons!

No Bull Barre Chords for Guitar
by James Shipway

Published by Headstock Books
headstockbooks.com

Paperback ISBN: 978-1-914453-20-5
Hardcover ISBN: 978-1-914453-22-9 / 978-1-914453-23-6
Ebook ISBN: 978-1-914453-21-2

Printed in Great Britain
by Amazon

15810483R00054